PLAY IT AGAIN, TOM

Also by Augustus Brown

WHY PANDAS DO HANDSTANDS

PLAY IT AGAIN, TOM

Curious Truths About Cats and Dogs

Augustus Brown

BANTAM PRESS

LONDON • TORONTO • SYDNEY • AUCKLAND • JOHANNESBURG

TRANSWORLD PUBLISHERS
61–63 Uxbridge Road, London W5 5SA
A Random House Group Company
www.rbooks.co.uk

First published in Great Britain
in 2007 by Bantam Press
an imprint of Transworld Publishers

A CIP catalogue record for this book
is available from the British Library.

ISBN 9780593059449

Addresses for Random House Group Ltd companies outside the UK
can be found at: www.randomhouse.co.uk
The Random House Group Ltd Reg. No. 954009

The Random House Group Ltd makes every effort to ensure that the papers
used in its books are made from trees that have been legally sourced from
well-managed and credibly certified forests. Our paper procurement policy
can be found at: www.randomhouse.co.uk/paper.htm

Typeset in 11/15pt Bell by
Falcon Oast Graphic Art Ltd.

Printed and bound in Great Britain by
Mackays of Chatham plc, Chatham, Kent

2 4 6 8 10 9 7 5 3 1

To Cilene, Gabriella and Thomas

CONTENTS

Contents

Preface

Ever since our favourite two animals first sidled up to our campfires 15,000 or so years ago, we humans have harboured all sorts of curious notions about cats and dogs.

In ancient Greece, for instance, dogs were regarded as geniuses. Plato, no less, called his dog 'a lover of learning' and 'a beast worthy of wonder', while Socrates once made an impassioned speech arguing that his pet was 'a true philosopher'.

Ancient Egyptians were in such awe of the self-contained and seemingly indestructible cat that they regarded it as a living god, to be worshipped accordingly. Travelling through Egypt, the historian Herodotus couldn't believe his eyes when he saw people lined up outside a row of blazing houses, all of them more concerned about stopping their cats getting too near the flames than they were anxious to save their belongings from going up in smoke.

Even until quite recently people associated both animals with extraordinary powers. As late as the nineteenth century the Chinese reckoned they could tell the time of day by the colour and intensity of the glow in a cat's eyes. In Eastern Europe some believed you could cure consumption by eating the flesh of a cat and wearing its skin on your chest. According to another old wives' tale from Greece, if you are about to choke on a bone you should let an unweaned puppy give you the kiss of life (unless it is a fishbone, in which case you should apply an unweaned kitten).

For many years science left dogs and cats to it, reserving its serious study for creatures in the 'natural' world rather than the 'man-made' ones that lay sleeping by our hearths. It was only towards the end of the twentieth century that biologists, zoologists, geneticists, ethologists and assorted other animal experts finally turned their attention to the most familiar members of the animal kingdom. When they did so, they discovered that cats and dogs are every bit as extraordinary as our ancient ancestors imagined them to be. Socrates, for certain, wouldn't have been amazed to learn that dogs do mathematics complex enough to have made even Pythagoras's head spin. Old wives across Europe would have nodded knowingly at the news that cats and dogs might possibly help humans manage illnesses from high blood pressure to asthma and epilepsy.

Eye-popping new insights into man's two best friends are now emerging on a regular basis. Thanks to DNA research, we know more than ever about who they are, where they came from, and how they think and behave. Today, for instance, we know that dogs are more closely related to sea-lions than they are to cats. We have evidence that cats and dogs may be able to sniff cancer and predict impending earthquakes, navigate huge distances using electromagnetism, perform impressive feats of memory and even create works of music and art.

This book is a collection of some of the weird, wonderful and occasionally unbelievable things we currently know about the two species. As with my previous book, *Why Pandas Do Handstands*, I've applied a simple principle to collating them. It is a collection intended to inform and educate but to entertain too. Consequently, while I have once more been scrupulous in providing sources for those who may want to dig deeper,

I have again refused to let pedantry get in the way too much.

So here they are in all their curious glory, *felis silvestris catus* and *canis familiaris*, better known to you and me as Kitty and Rover.

Augustus Brown
London

PLAY IT AGAIN, TOM

PART ONE

Sense and Scent Ability

How Cats and Dogs Smell,
Hear, See and Feel

NO WONDER OUR ANCIENT ANCESTORS recruited cats and dogs on to their domestic staff. Like four-legged FBI agents, they are armed with super-sensitive surveillance equipment capable of tracking down prey and providing early-warning systems to fend off predators.

Dogs, it seems, are capable of sniffing everything from electricity to ovulating animals, while cats can operate in pitch dark and tune in to the ultrasonic singing of even the quietest of mice. And it doesn't end there: both seem capable of predicting everything from hurricanes to earthquakes, epileptic fits to cancers.

You Stink, Therefore I Am

How Cats and Dogs Smell

Dogs can smell human fingerprints that are a week old.

Their noses are so sensitive that they can even smell electricity. While conducting an experiment, a researcher found that a dog could smell which of two compartments contained an electric current. He concluded this was because the charge resulted in the release of tiny amounts of ozone that the dog could detect.

Dogs can tell from the smell of a cow's urine whether it is in oestrus, or heat. Farmers train them to do this so they know the best time to introduce a bull for breeding.

Smell is the first sense that a cat develops. It can pick up the aroma of its mother's mammary glands at birth and within two days is reacting to odours that it finds offensive. Among the things it can learn to dislike, if exposed to the smell of them early on, are mothballs.

The nose pad of a cat is ridged in a pattern that is unique, just like the fingerprint of a human.

Dogs really can smell fear. If a dog goes into a room where a frightened dog has just left, it will appear anxious and agitated. This isn't, as many would claim, some kind of ESP-type response. It's caused by a scent, an alarm pheromone, which is produced by the anal glands of frightened dogs.

DOGS CAN detect odours that are up to 40 feet underground. They have been used to detect leaky gas pipes. They can also smell insects embedded in the ground or in woodwork. In the United States dogs are used to sniff out termite infestations.

DOGS CAN also pick up the faintest whiff of other creatures. On the island of Guam, the US Department of Agriculture's Wildlife Services use specially trained Jack Russells to sniff out brown tree snakes in the loading bays of aeroplanes.

THE SOURCE of the dog's exceptional ability to smell is its wet snout. The moist leathery surface of the snout acts like velcro, catching even the tiniest molecules of smells, then dissolving them so that the dog's internal smell-receptor cells can analyse them properly. To keep its nose wet a dog must produce a constant supply of mucus through the nasal cavities. Scientists reckon the average dog produces a pint of this mucus every day.

SMELL IS the dog's dominant sense – so much so that a

huge part of its brain is devoted to analysing odours. Dogs have two giant olfactory bulbs attached to the brain that decode every smell they encounter. The bulbs weigh around 60 grams, four times as much as human olfactory bulbs. Given that a canine brain is one tenth the size of a human one, that means the canine has forty times more of its brain devoted to smell than we do.

Little wonder, then, that a dog's sense of smell is reckoned to be 100,000 times better than a human's. In tests dogs have been able to pick up chemical solutions that form one or two parts in a trillion. That is the equivalent of smelling one bad apple in two billion barrels.

THE CAT'S olfactory bulb contains 67 million cells. This is less than a dog's, which has hundreds of millions. But it is 15 million more than a human's has.

A YOUNG kitten that becomes distressed by being removed from its litter will automatically crawl towards anything that carries the smell of its former home and fall asleep.

BOTH DOGS and cats have an extrasensory organ located between the nose and the mouth. Called the vomeronasal organ, it detects chemicals in a similar way to the nose, but unlike the nose it must usually be in direct contact with the chemical. Dogs and cats probably use it to recognize each other's smell, among other things. (Interestingly, the human foetus also has a version of this organ, but it regresses during development and most scientists think that it doesn't function at all in adults.)

DOGS REACT in different ways to different smells. In tests, for example, it has been found that dogs relax when the aroma of lavender is fed into their environment. Camomile also makes dogs calmer. Rosemary and peppermint, on the other hand, make dogs more excited.

CATS ALSO respond to different smells. The smell of nutmeg makes them less bored, researchers discovered.

In general, cats prefer to be in an environment with lots of smells. Even the odour of animals that are traditionally their prey relieves their boredom.

AS FAR as dogs are concerned, every human has a unique smell. They can pick people out according to their body, and other, odours. Scientists think the only occasion a dog can't tell two people apart is if they are identical twins on identical diets who remain silent.

As a result of this, dogs can track human smells over long distances. Scientists think they can pick up on the difference in odours from different footprints to work out which direction their prey is headed. They can do this twenty minutes after a person has passed by even though the footprints are made a single second apart.

Scientists who tested four German Shepherds discovered they track footprints by dividing the job into three phases. During the first, search phase they move quickly, sniffing ten to twenty times each breath. Once they have detected the smell they enter the deciding phase, when they sniff at between two and five specific footprints. They do this for a longer period, slowing down as they do so. Finally, once the direction has been established, the tracking phase begins.

The reason why dogs have black noses was probably originally to protect them from sunburn.

The Cat's Whispers

How Felines and Canines Tune In to the World Around Them

CATS HAVE more than twenty muscles in their external ears, or pinnae. As a result they can move each ear independently of the other, using them to identify rapidly and also to amplify sounds. They can also move their bodies in one direction while pointing their ears in another.

CATS CAN pinpoint the source of sounds with amazing accuracy. From 1 metre away, a cat can tell the difference between two identical sound sources that are only 8 centimetres apart.

Cats are capable of hearing a greater range of frequencies than virtually any other mammal. A cat can hear across 10.5 octaves, in comparison with a human's range, which is nearer 8 octaves. They can hear between 35 kilohertz and 250 kilohertz. This means they can even detect the ultrasonic sounds made by rodents. This is why they sometimes locate and pounce on a mouse without actually seeing it in advance.

The adult cat's ability to distinguish other animals' sounds is so highly developed that scientists think it can tell the difference between the squeak of a mouse and that of a shrew.

Many owners think their cat somehow senses their arrival home in the family car. The truth is more likely to

be that its ultrasonic hearing allows it to recognize the signature high-frequency sound of the owner's car well in advance of its arrival within human earshot.

USING THEIR swivelling ears like radar dishes, dogs can locate the source of a sound in 6/100ths of a second. They are able to hear sounds 250 yards (230 metres) away that a human would only detect at 25 yards (23 metres). Depending on the volume of the noise, the upper limit of a dog's hearing varies between 26 kilohertz and 100 kilohertz, well above a human's upper limit.

DOGS CAN hear both ultra- and subsonic sound. Bigger dogs with larger heads and wider ear openings tend to be better at hearing subsonic sounds, which is why breeds like the Saint Bernard are so good at hearing deep, low-resonance noises emanating from underneath snow. Smaller dogs are better at hearing high-frequency sounds, which is why smaller breeds are more sensitive to high-pitched noises.

WHAT'S BLUE, PUSSYCAT?

How Cats and Dogs See

BECAUSE OF its history as a predator, the dog has eyes that are designed to operate at their best in low lighting. As with humans', their retinas are made up of a mixture of rod and cone photoreceptors, but with the emphasis more on rods, which work much better in dim light. Cones control colour vision and require bright light.

As a result of this, dogs need only about one quarter of the light that humans do to see things at night.

THE CAT too has evolved from a predator, and retains many of the characteristics that makes its closest animal relatives, the big cats, among nature's most efficient and ruthless hunters.

The elliptical pupil of a cat's eye allows it also to see in a greater range of light conditions than we can. In addition, its slitty shape means that cats can squint better than those of us with round eyes, allowing them to protect their eyes better in bright light. This cleverly designed instrument has another smart feature too. Rather than just one focal point in their lens, cats have several, which means that, unlike humans, they still get a very sharp image in low light.

CAT'S EYES shine when they get caught in the beam of a light. This is because of a mirror-like membrane at the back of the retina called the tapetum lucidum, which reflects the light back through the retina. This, combined with the efficiency of their elliptical pupils, means they need only a seventh of the light required by humans to see in the dark.

CATS CAN be used as rudimentary clocks. The colour and glow of the pupils of cats' eyes change according to the course of the sun.

SIAMESE CATS are often born with double vision. This is why they squint. It is their way of trying to correct what is a genetic defect.

Cats have great peripheral vision. This means that in good light they rarely need to focus. Instead they remain wide-eyed, looking as if they are staring into space. This is probably why cats seem so aloof.

The cat family is reckoned to have the best binocular vision of all mammals. The position of their eyes, placed at the front and high up on the skull, allows them to judge distances with great accuracy.

Domestic cats are slightly near-sighted. Feral cats, however, tend to be long-sighted. No one has yet explained why.

Cats have a blind spot, right under their nose. This explains why they can't find tidbits on the floor.

Dogs aren't colour-blind; they just don't see the range of colours that other species, such as humans, do. A study of dogs concluded that they see a range of colours predominantly made up of yellows and blues. So rather than a rainbow of red, orange, yellow, green, blue, indigo and violet, a dog sees an arc of very dark grey, dark yellow or brown, light yellow, grey, light blue and dark blue.

What's Blue, Pussycat?

WHEN PRESENTED with different shades of grey, dogs are only about half as good as humans at telling the difference between them.

CATS CAN see limited amounts of colour. The central area of their retinas has a patch of cones that is capable of detecting colour in daylight conditions. Experiments have shown that they can see green, blue and possibly red. However, scientists think the colours are much less saturated than those we humans can see.

DOGS CAN detect flickering lights at a high frequency. Unlike humans, for whom flashing lights blend into one at a frequency of between 50 and 60 hertz, dogs can keep seeing flickering up to a frequency of 70 hertz. This is why they don't always show much interest in television, which – at least, in its pre-digital form – consists of a series of fast-moving lines. What appears to us as a steady stream of images appears to them as little more than a rapidly flickering and generally meaningless collection of shapes and lights.

BOTH CATS and dogs are equipped with windscreen wipers. The canine and feline eye is equipped with a third eyelid – also known as the haw or nictitating membrane –

which automatically moves up and down, sweeping the eye clean on a regular basis. The third eyelid isn't normally visible but if the gland attached to it is inflamed it can show as a red swelling. (Hence the condition's nickname when dogs suffer it: 'cherry eye'.)

Dogs have, on average, 20 : 75 vision – that is, they can see only from a distance of 20 feet fine details that a person with good eyesight can see from 75 feet away.

Dogs have a large blind spot behind their heads. The size of this depends on the size of the dog's head and so varies enormously from breed to breed. While the blind spot in a narrow-headed Borzoi is only 70 degrees, in the wider-headed Pekingese it is 140 degrees, leaving it much more vulnerable to attacks from behind.

Dogs also don't have great 'depth of field' to their vision. Because they have such large pupils, when they look at things that are distant they see only the objects in the centre of the image in focus. Everything else in the image appears fuzzy.

While dogs may not be able to see behind them or in fine detail, they can see things at great distances –

especially if they are moving. A test of fourteen police dogs found that they could recognize a moving object almost ½ mile (900 metres) away; if it was stationary, just over 600 yards (585 metres).

I Feel Kitty

How Cats and Dogs Touch and Feel

CATS' AND dogs' sense of touch is concentrated around their snouts, where they both have four sets of highly sensitive whiskers, or vibrissae. The vibrissae are positioned next to the snout and the eyes, in front of and below the ears. Dogs have an extra set of vibrissae, called the inter-ramal tuft, which is positioned under the chin. Scientists think this helps them compensate for the relative weakness of their eyesight at close range and allows them to identify and pick up small objects on the floor. Cats don't have these whiskers, probably because they tend not to carry their heads close to the ground.

Cats also have vibrissae on their front paws. Scientists

think they were specially designed to help catch prey.

Cats use their vibrissae to determine if a space is too small to squeeze through.

MALE DOGS tend to be left-pawed, while females favour their front right paw. In a study at the University of Bari, Italy, a group of eighty dogs had a piece of adhesive paper stuck to their snouts. Males tended to use their left paw to remove the paper; females used their right more

often. This was backed up by another study at Queen's University, Belfast. They tested fifty-three dogs and found the same thing.

Cats, on the other hand, are generally left-pawed. Studies found that 20 per cent of cats favoured their right paws when carrying out complicated, manipulatory tasks, while a little over 38 per cent favoured their left. The remaining 42 per cent were ambidextrous.

The pads of a dog's feet are equipped with sensory nerves that respond to vibration. Researchers think this allows the dog when running to check how stable the surface beneath it is. Some scientists even think the sensors act as a speedometer, allowing the dog to measure how fast it is travelling.

Puppies have special, heat-seeking sensors in their noses. The tiny receptors, tucked inside the young dogs' nostrils and nasal passages, are sensitive to heat that is radiated in the form of infrared energy, which comes in handy during their blind, early days. The sensors compensate for the puppy's lack of eyesight and help it find its mother if it becomes separated from her during its first weeks. A disconnected puppy swings its head around, sniffing the air, to find a heat trail that leads it back to its mother's teat. The sensors stop functioning in older dogs.

WHY WAS the cat on a hot tin roof? Probably because it couldn't feel the heat. Cats are relatively insensitive to surface temperature. Humans feel pain if they touch something at 44 degrees centigrade, but cats don't until about 52 degrees.

HOW HOT is that doggie in the window? It's hard to tell because dogs sweat through their feet. This is why, during hot weather, they leave damp patches where they have been standing. They also sweat through glands in their tail, ears and anus.

Their limited ability to cool themselves down means dogs are vulnerable to overheating. If temperatures rise sharply, the dog's inability to sweat combined with the thickness of its coat can severely limit its ability to dissipate the heat. If left in a confined, glass-lined space, such as a car, for instance, a dog can die within twenty minutes.

CATS LICK themselves to protect against both the cold and excessive heat. In cold weather, licking helps to keep their fur smooth so that it functions as a more efficient layer of insulation. In hot weather, licking compensates for the cat's lack of sweat glands and helps to cool down the fur.

Is It Raining, Cats and Dogs?

Canine and Feline Superpowers

Dogs can detect cancer. Scientists think that simply by sniffing samples of human breath, dogs can detect lung, breast and other cancers with an accuracy rate of between 88 and 97 per cent. The accuracy rate of a multi-million-pound hospital scanner is between 85 and 90 per cent.

Dogs can be trained to alert people with heart conditions when they are about to suffer a seizure. They can also learn to anticipate, and give warning, when a person is going to have an epileptic fit.

A Canadian study found that dogs who lived with children prone to epileptic episodes behaved unusually in advance of the attacks. Some dogs would lick the child's face or act protectively. One dog even guided a young girl away from a set of stairs shortly before she had an attack. The dogs' warnings came as early as five hours before the first symptoms of the epileptic episode were visible.

Health authorities around the world are now training 'seizure alert' or 'seizure response' dogs, some of which can predict fits, and all of which will respond in an appropriate way when an owner does have a fit. Some will be trained to stay with and guard the owner, and some even learn to press a button on a phone that dials the emergency services.

CATS MAY also have the ability to sense epileptic fits. The owner of a cat called Tee Cee, from Yorkshire, was prone to complex epilepsy and could suffer seizures without warning. But he and his family discovered that Tee Cee would begin staring at him strangely prior to his having an attack.

The cat was soon successfully predicting seizures. It also learned to alert other family members if their relative was having an attack and slipped out of consciousness.

IT REMAINS a mystery how both animals are able to sense epilepsy in this way. Some think they pick up on tiny behavioural or scent cues. Others are convinced it is a reaction to electrical activity in the body. But the fact that dogs also respond to psychological seizures, which are non-epileptic and don't display abnormal electrical activity, casts doubt on these theories.

CATS HAVE, historically, been regarded as valuable weather forecasters. In China it was believed that if a cat winked rain was coming, while in Scotland a cat scratching at a chair leg was a portent of gales. Nowhere was a cat relied on more heavily for its meteorological abilities than at sea. For centuries cats were a sailor's best guide to what lay ahead. Sending a cat up a mast was seen as a way of scaring off storm demons, and sticking the ship's chief mouser under an iron pot was regarded as a fool-proof method of raising a wind when the vessel became becalmed. Beneath all this superstition, however, there may lie a little scientific sense.

Thanks to their ultra-sensitive vibrissae and the vestibular system within their inner ears, cats are extremely sensitive to air pressure. The odd behaviour they display as air pressure fluctuates may reflect these instruments' reactions to changing conditions. Studies have found they become sensitive to sudden noises in the immediate run-up to storms, suggesting they are expecting cracks of lightning and rumbles of thunder.

DOGS TOO are particularly sensitive to changes in the weather. Some get agitated by events associated with storms, such as wind, rain, drops in barometric pressure, ionization and odours.

As with cats, dogs also get nervous about noises during these periods. A major study at Texas A&M University looked at the behaviour of 258 dogs over a period of sixteen years. A large proportion of the dogs, 106 in all, were disturbed by thunder-like noises.

CATS AND dogs may be able to sense an imminent earthquake. The Greek historian Thucydides was probably the first writer to notice dogs had this power. He described how, days before a cataclysmic earthquake flattened the city of Helice, dogs – along with rats, snakes and weasels – abandoned the place in their droves. Thucydides was convinced the dogs knew what was coming and had run for their lives.

In the USA a study found that seventeen out of fifty homes near the scene of a Californian quake in 1977 reported odd behaviour in their animals. Evidence ranged from a cat pacing around and fidgeting during its normal nap time to a normally placid dog whining excitedly. Studies in the Mojave desert in the USA also found that dogs barked at small aftershocks that went unnoticed by humans but were picked up by seismometers.

BEFORE THE Asian tsunami struck on 26 December 2004 many dogs refused to go for their daily walks near the sea.

SOME CATS' hair stands on end in the run-up to earthquakes. This has led some scientists to wonder whether they are responding to electrostatic charges in the atmosphere. Other theories suggest they are reacting to electromagnetic fields, air pressure, ultrasonic soundwaves, rises in water levels or even gaseous emissions from the earth.

Big-headed dogs don't hear earthquakes coming. In February 2001, Stanley Coren, a scientist studying the seasonal behaviour of a group of 193 dogs in Vancouver, Canada, noticed almost half of them behaving anxiously or being highly active. The following day an earthquake of 6.8 magnitude hit the Pacific Northwest, with its epicentre in Washington state, 240 kilometres south of Vancouver. When he looked at the data in more detail, Coren saw that those who had reacted to the oncoming disaster were dogs that could hear high-frequency sounds better than the others.

Only one of the dogs within his group with hearing difficulties had responded. (This one had reacted to the anxiety of his housemate, who didn't have hearing problems.) Dogs with floppy ears had shown only half the levels of anxiety. Coren also saw that dogs with smaller heads, which – as we have noted – are known to be able to hear high-frequency sounds, had shown much more odd behaviour.

Coren concluded that dogs are tuning into high-frequency sounds, such as rocks scraping together underground. He also concluded that dogs with smaller heads are more likely to hear earthquakes.

DOGS ARE able to sense gunfire. A major study of dog behaviour during the bloody siege of Sarajevo observed odd behaviour in dogs in advance of mortar and artillery fire beginning. A significant proportion of the sampled dogs – around 57 per cent – hid their heads under tables, chairs or other pieces of furniture, while 35 per cent crawled under beds or tables. One in seven dogs, around 14 per cent, jumped into their owner's arms, while over one in five, 21 per cent, whined as if to warn their owners that shelling was about to start. The most remarkable discovery came when the researchers analysed the behaviour of dogs out walking with their owners. Almost 72 per cent of them physically dragged their owners away. In many instances, the study found, the dogs successfully moved their owners from the artillery's firing line.

SOME SCIENTISTS argue that cats and dogs may possess telepathic powers. One maverick researcher, Rupert Sheldrake, for instance, cites hundreds of examples of cats and dogs who seemingly know when their owners are coming home. His case histories include a Norwegian cat belonging to a social worker and midwife who works unpredictable hours and returns home at all times of the day. Whatever the time of her return, minutes before she walks through the door the cat rushes to the window and sits on the sill, alerting the husband to put the kettle on. He also cites a cat called Whiskins, belonging to a professor at the University of California in Berkeley, that can apparently tell when its owner is phoning home. Whiskins takes the receiver off the hook and begins making meowing noises down the line. When it isn't the master who's ringing, Whiskins ignores the call.

Sheldrake believes these animals are influenced by 'morphic fields', a bond that ties social groups together not just physically but on an unconscious psychological level too. He argues morphic fields are made up of collective experience and memories and that they explain, for instance, why creatures such as fish, birds, turtles and seals migrate thousands of miles to the same breeding grounds each year. According to his theories, when individuals leave a group the morphic field stretches, like elastic, so that the members of the group are still connected. So even though a cat's or dog's owner has left home, pet and person remain connected on a psychological level and somehow communicate their movements to each other.

Dogs are better than cats at telling when their owners

are coming home, Sheldrake argues. Out of 1,200 households surveyed, 91 said their cats possessed this gift, while 177 said their dog displayed it.

The mainstream scientific community are sceptical about Sheldrake's theories. To test them one independent study was carried out on a dog called Jay Tee, a terrier with a supposedly uncanny ability to know when its owner was setting off and arriving home. According to the dog's owners Jay Tee would always go to the window when the mother of the family was heading home. When the team videotaped Jay Tee over a long period of time, however, they discovered that the terrier 'constantly' went to the window throughout the day. The researchers concluded that it would have been more surprising if Jay Tee hadn't been at the window when she arrived home.

CATS SEEM to hypnotize other creatures. A prominent scientist, J. McNair Wright, once described in the journal *Science* how he watched a cat mesmerize a bird.

'The cat placed itself on the outside sill of my window, near to a pine tree. A bird presently lit on the pine tree, no doubt not observing the cat,' Mr Wright observed. 'The cat fixed its attention on the bird. The cat's eyes were widely opened and shone with a peculiar brightness; its head was raised and intent, the fur on its neck and about its face slowly stood up, as if electrified. Except for this rising of the fur, and a certain intensity of life in the whole attitude of the beast, it was as still as if cut from stone. The bird quivered, trembled, looked fixedly at the cat, and finally, with a feeble shake of the wings, fell towards the cat, which bounded to seize it.'

Contemporary scientists are sceptical. They think it more likely that cats exhibit the intense type of behaviour described by McNair Wright when they are calculating the distance to their prey and readying themselves to pounce. Quite why the bird fell off its tree, however, remains a mystery.

DOGS, ON the other hand, seem to be susceptible to hypnosis by other animals. In the classic travelogue *The Naturalist on the River Amazon* the scientist Henry Walter Bates described seeing a dog being hypnotized by a snake. The small pet had set out to attack a rattlesnake. But no sooner had it headed towards it than the snake had started to weave its sinister magic. Bates described how 'the snake fixed its eyes on the dog, erected its tail and shook its rattle; it seemed in no haste to seize the dog but as if waiting to put the dog into a more suitable condition for being seized'. The dog was soon frozen to the spot, unable to attack or retreat. It was eventually dragged to safety by its owner.

PART TWO

What's the Dog for Cat?

The Curious Truth About Canine and Feline Communication

CATS AND DOGS CHAT AWAY incessantly – in their own particular way, of course. Studies of the assorted barks, whines, hisses and purrs our best friends emit have revealed some surprising truths. Dogs, for instance, have a word for cats and a special whine to signify sexual frustration. Kittens have their own, unique, high-frequency language, while adult cats can produce a sound much like a human gargling. But the most surprising news is that cats and dogs talk in subtler ways than we'd previously imagined. They rub, scratch, spray and even, er, dump their news.

SNAP, GURGLE AND PUFF

Pet Sounds and What They Really Mean

A DOG'S bark lasts, on average, for 0.2 seconds.

A BEAGLE was once recorded barking 907 times in ten minutes.

HUNGRY CATS have been known to meow at the rate of two per minute for more than two hours non-stop.

PURRING IS one of the very few natural sounds produced while an animal is breathing in as well as out.

Cats can purr continuously for up to two hours.

According to a study, only two out of three dogs bark during the night.

Sleeping dogs are more alert to the sound of other dogs barking than any other sound.

Dogs living in groups are more likely to bark than dogs living on their own.

A dog's bark can be just as bad as its bite. In Japan, a doctor treated two cases of middle-aged men who had suddenly and inexplicably lost hearing in the lower-frequency ranges. He discovered that both had suffered from acoustic trauma and been permanently damaged by a large dog barking loudly into their ears.

The Basenji is the only breed of dog that never barks. It does, however, yodel.

A distant relative, the yodelling dingo, which lives in the primitive eastern highlands of New Guinea, produces a blood-curdling cry that has predictably enshrined it in tribal myth. It's said that the dingo harbours the souls of the dead, and the living can communicate with their lost loved ones by singing along with the creature.

Dogs can tell a lot from the tone of each other's growls. Researchers have found that the bigger the dog, the more narrowly spaced the formants in its growl and therefore the harsher it sounds, compared with the growl of a weaker dog. They think this passes on a lot of information about how capable the bigger dogs are of inflicting injuries on their smaller adversaries.

Among feral dogs, different sounds produce different responses. Howls gather dogs to one location. Whimpers encourage dogs to look after each other.

Some dogs have a word for cat.

The South American Maku tribe use dogs to aid them during hunting. The dogs learn to signal with the type of bark they emit what type of prey they are hunting. They have distinctive barks for different animals, including the agouti, peccary, pacca, tapir and jaguar.

Adult cats can make up to a dozen different types of call. For the first three weeks of their life, however, kittens are limited to only four distinct sounds: they can spit, purr, deliver their own version of a meow, and they also produce a distinctive call to let their mother know that they are cold.

Cats have a secret, high-frequency alarm signal. At the time when more mature kittens become old enough to leave a mother cat's nest, they produce distress calls of extremely high frequencies that humans and many other species cannot hear. These calls reach up to 80 kilohertz (humans can hear up to 22 kilohertz at most). The mother cat replies with calls that are slightly lower but still beyond the range of our hearing.

In the wild, only puppies bark. Wolves, foxes, jackals, coyotes and other members of the domestic dog's extended family use other vocalizations when they become adults. They whine, howl and whimper but they very rarely bark.

Wild cats usually don't meow either, although, again, young kittens do. Researchers think domestic cats continue meowing into adulthood purely to get attention from their human owners.

Puppies can't bark until they are between two and four weeks old. During the first weeks of their life they whine and whimper instead, usually to signal distress. A whimper lasts on average for a second, but extremely agitated puppies have been known to cry out at the rate of one hundred whimpers per minute.

DOGS PUFF. They make the noise by pushing air through their partly opened mouths. Puffing is a signal of mild aggression. Dogs hiss through their noses. It is believed this is a signal of a perceived threat.

DOGS MAKE a snapping sound by quickly shutting their jaws and hitting their teeth together. Researchers think it is a defence signal used when dogs feel under threat.

MALE DOGS have a special whine that signals sexual frustration. They use it when they see a pair of dogs having sex or when around a whelping female. They also use it when they are refused sex by a female in heat.

CATS MAKE a range of sounds, each conveying different signals. In general they signal territorial aggression by growling, howling and snarling and defensiveness by spitting and hissing. The meow, trill and chirrup sounds signal greetings. Cats also gurgle. Scientists think this is a signal of friendship.

A cat's murmur is a request or greeting, while a purr is believed to be a social sound normally indicating submission. A purr can also be a signal of distress. Vets have observed cats purring continuously when chronically ill or in pain.

Cats chatter their teeth when they hunt, some scientists think to practise the biting they will do when they reach their prey. Cats yawn as a reaction to smells they don't recognize. They also make squeaking sounds during play and in anticipation of mealtimes. Females also squeak after sex.

Cats have worked out that they can get the attention of humans by producing a particularly annoying meow. A scientist named Nicholas Nicastro played one hundred cat vocalizations to volunteers, and asked them to rate how pleasant they sounded. He then asked a different group how urgent the same meows sounded. He concluded that the most urgent meows were also the most unpleasant. These vocalizations had more energy in the lower frequencies producing a mee-*o-o-o-o-o-w*-type sound.

In 2001, Japanese researchers claimed to have cracked the canine code and translated, for the first time, the dog's repertoire of barks and howls.

The team, made up of a vet and an acoustics expert, attached microphones to the collars of their sample dogs, then recorded the wave patterns associated with six different emotional states, from sadness and happiness to alarm and self-awareness. Using the results of their studies, they built a 'bow lingual' device that translated dogs' yelps and whines into the written word. The scientific community greeted the results with scepticism – so much so that the inventors were dismissed as barking mad and awarded an infamous Ig Nobel Prize, for mad science.

The inventors had the last laugh, however. They teamed up with a Japanese electronics firm and built a

simple household version of their device that translated dog sounds into phrases, from 'I can't stand it' to 'How boring'. It sold in its thousands, first in Japan, then around the world. Inevitably, a cat translator followed.

Have I Got Poohs for You

How Actions Speak Louder Than Words

Dogs talk through their backsides. They have anal sacs located in their rear quarters, containing a mixture of pungent fatty acids. When a dog defecates, the muscles around its anus squeeze out a few drops of this cocktail on to the stool. Scientists think the discharge contains complex information that other dogs then check out when they pass the deposited stool. You could call it poetry in motion.

No one has yet tackled the question of whether this means pooper scoopers and dog poo bags are infringing on dogs' free-speech rights.

Dogs cock their legs to urinate for a good reason. Urine is a powerful signalling device and by directing its discharge as high as it can up a tree, lamp-post or fence a dog is giving other dogs the best possible chance to notice it. In the wild, dogs go to even greater lengths to place their urine marks as high as possible. When having a wee, female bushdogs do a handstand.

Tomcats spray urine all around their territory. Scientists think they are effectively posting messages on a noticeboard.

Cats are highly aware of each other's territories and actively avoid entering another cat's home space if possible. A bit like graffiti artists, the toms spray landmarks with messages letting other cats know whether or not they are 'at home'.

All adult tomcats produce their own distinctive scent, which is attractive to females. However, the males can't produce this without having the right components in their diet. Scientists think this has evolved so as to provide females with telltale information about a male's condition for breeding purposes.

When cats rub themselves against objects they leave a

pungent aroma that is filled with information for fellow cats. By sniffing a female's rub mark, for instance, a male can tell not only the sex of the cat that has left the secretion, but also how fertile she is at that precise moment.

CATS ALSO send messages via a scratch-and-sniff code. They have sebaceous glands located right between their digits. When felines scratch things, they also leave a scent that conveys lots of information.

CATS MAY physically write each other messages too. When a cat scratches a tree to leave a scent marking, it also leaves a visual signal for other cats. Cats don't just scratch trees on the boundary of their home ground, which suggests their object is more subtle than simple territorial marking. Some scientists think this is an additional piece of information through which cats communicate.

Cats also scrape the ground at times when they are not simply covering up urine or faeces. This too suggests they are leaving visual signals as well as aromatic ones.

HAPPY DOGS wag to the right. A study of how dogs respond to different stimuli was conducted by Italian neuroscientists at the University of Trieste and vets at the University of Bari. Over a period of a month, they watched a group of thirty dogs respond when they were briefly joined in turn by their owner, an unfamiliar human, a cat or an unfamiliar dominant dog, a Belgian Shepherd. To the scientists' surprise, the dogs' tails wagged vigorously to the right when they were shown their owners and much less so when they saw the unfamiliar human. The cat brought about a small wag to the right, but the dominant Belgian Shepherd sparked a sharp move to the left. The scientists concluded that the muscles in the right side of the tail reflect positive emotions, while those on the left express more negative feelings.

Cats signal friendship by sticking their tails up in the air. Scientists think this might be a rare case of a behaviour that has evolved since the domestic cat started living with humans. In the wild, cats only raise their tails into an upright position in order to spray urine. A household cat, however, adopts this position for long periods of time while it conducts friendly rubbing with another cat.

Cats can signal that they want to play with one another by extending a paw, with claws retracted and no signalling of aggression.

MUCH OF a cat's aggressive body language is designed to give the impression it is bigger than it is, thus scaring off its opponent. An aggressive cat will stand as erect as it can. It will also 'piloerect', raising the hairs on its back so that its body looks bulkier.

Conversely, a cat will make itself look as small as possible to signal its withdrawal from an aggressive situation. It will lie flat on the ground, withdraw its head into its shoulders and flatten its ears to minimize its perceived size.

Both dogs and cats conduct staring matches. Breaking eye contact is a sign of subordination, so cats and dogs test each other in order to achieve dominance. The dog or cat that blinks or looks away first is the loser and consequently ranked lower.

Cats blink to signal that they are not scrutinizing the subject of their gaze in an aggressive way.

Dogs puff themselves up to look tough. Like cats, dogs faced with an aggressive situation try to create the impression they are bigger than they really are.

Faced by a rival, dogs will initially shift their weight forward in order to appear more bulky, then stiffen their legs to make them look as long as possible. They will also elevate their head, neck and ears and – just like cats – 'piloerect' their hair to make their bodies look bigger.

They will also lift their tail up high, sometimes vibrating it back and forth as if to taunt their opponent.

Dogs know, however, when it is time to stop acting the hero. When a fight is about to break out, they will shrink themselves down again to protect their throats and ears from injury.

Dogs show dominance over other dogs by using body language. As the area most commonly attacked when dogs fight, the neck is often the object of this behaviour.

A higher-ranking dog may place its head or its forelimbs on a lower-ranking dog's neck or shoulders. If the lower-ranking dog is submissive, the dominant dog may even place its muzzle or head in the other's mouth.

Dogs win confrontations by confusing their enemies. When attacked by fierce predators, dog breeds that guard livestock rarely fight back with violence. Instead, they confuse their opponent by acting oddly, performing a repertoire of barking, tail-wagging, social-greeting and play behaviours. Usually, the predator is so taken aback by the inappropriate behaviour it capitulates.

PART THREE

Who's a Clever Boy, Then?

Some Truths About Canine and Feline Intelligence

TO ANYONE WHO HAS EVER spent time around them, it seems obvious that dogs must be able to perform mental tasks more taxing than fetching a stick. Cats, too, are clearly capable of meeting challenges beyond unfurling a ball of wool or catching a mouse. Both are indeed capable of rather impressive feats of memory, mathematics and logic. They are also, frankly, able to display levels of common sense and initiative that would put many humans to shame.

Dogs Remember, Cats Don't Forget

Mental Agility

Dogs have better short-term memories than cats, according to one test at least. Both are good at finding an object they have seen someone hide behind one of four boxes if they are allowed to find it straight away. Cats tend to get it right 75 per cent of the time. Both puppies and kittens can do this when they are as young as five or six weeks old.

Adults' relative ability to remember where the object has been hidden changes dramatically if they are made to wait, however. After waiting for just thirty seconds, cats choose the wrong box 70 per cent of the time. Dogs, on the other hand, even after a pause of four minutes, can still correctly identify 60 per cent of the time which of the four boxes the object is hidden behind.

Intriguingly, however, cats performed much better in another memory test. In this experiment, cats and dogs were presented with a large number of boxes and shown that food could be found under those with a lighted lamp on top. After a while both learned to go to the correct box when the lamps were turned on briefly. However, when the researchers removed the animals from the experiment for a period of time, they discovered different results. After more than five minutes, dogs had forgotten about the lamps and would head for empty boxes once more. Cats, on the other hand, returned to the right boxes as long as sixteen hours later. Their performance in this test beat that of monkeys.

Dogs remember their master's voice – and face too. Scientists think that when dogs hear their owner's voice, they recall his or her face, in a similar way to how, if we were to hear a familiar voice, we would think of the person whose voice it was. When dogs in Japan were played a recording of their owner's voice, and immediately shown a picture of a stranger on a monitor, they looked at the picture for significantly longer than if the picture was of their owner. The researchers think that this was because the dogs were surprised to see a stranger's face in association with their owner's voice. This also worked the other way round: if the voice was of a stranger and the picture was of the owner, they also looked for longer than if the stranger's picture was shown.

THE SCIENTIFIC history books are filled with examples of dogs with supposedly prodigious abilities. Some actually turned out to be genuine.

The eminent Victorian naturalist John Lubbock carried out a demonstration with his poodle Van at the Royal Society in which the dog was invited to choose from various cards with written words on them. Van would receive whatever was written on the card he selected. To the audience's delight the dog almost always chose the card that read food. It didn't, as Lubbock argued, prove that the dog could read. But it was early evidence of the dog's excellent ability to remember associations between symbols and rewards.

Another famous dog with an ability to remember associations was Fellow, the pet of Jacob Herbert from Detroit. Herbert had spoken to Fellow as if he was a child all his life and as a result he claimed to have trained the dog to remember four hundred words. Scientists were sceptical but when they were given a demonstration they saw him respond correctly to a range of commands from 'Go and find the cook' to 'Look up high at the squirrel'. When Herbert said 'I have lost my gloves' Fellow would start searching until he found them. Again, this proved not that the dog understood English but that he had been able to memorize a sequence of words and associate each of them with the correct response.

Cats can also perform similar feats of memory, although their owners often claim they are doing something even more complex.

A cream-coloured Persian cat from Dubai, Cuty Boy, first showed his talent for arithmetic when he was a kitten. From an early age he could signal yes and no, left and right, by bumping his nose on the ground. He could also count up to twenty by nudging the floor in the same way.

As he grew older, Cuty Boy progressed to more difficult arithmetic by choosing from numbered cards. Given addition, subtraction, division and multiplication sums, he would twitch his tail and look at the card with the right answer. Controversy surrounds his true abilities, however. A senior Middle Eastern mathematician expressed his faith in Cuty Boy's gifts but others argued he was simply a genius at reading his human owners' body language so that he knew what answers to give.

Cuty Boy's owners added to this suspicion by claiming the cat could perform the trick in eight different languages, including Gujarati, Persian, Arabic, English and French.

THE MOST remarkable dog of the early twenty-first century is undoubtedly a Border Collie called Rico, the subject of extensive testing at the illustrious Max Planck Institute in Germany. Rico has been asked to perform many tests over the years. In one of the first he was asked to pick two toys from a choice of ten, each of which was given a unique word. Invited to do this on twenty occasions, Rico correctly fetched 37 of the 40 toys he was asked to collect. Even more impressively, he successfully completed the task a month later, correctly getting 50 per cent of the toys.

What made Rico exceptional, however, was that unlike other clever dogs such as Van and Fellow he also demonstrated an ability to understand unfamiliar phrases too.

In a later test researchers placed a new toy, a white rabbit, in among his usual toys. When Rico was told to 'fetch the bunny' – a phrase he had never heard before – by a process of elimination he worked out that, since he knew the names of everything else, the 'bunny' must be the one unfamiliar object. As with the earlier tests, he also remembered this for a long time. When he was again asked to fetch the bunny four weeks later, he picked it out of a group of nine toys, three times out of six attempts.

Female dogs have a lower boredom threshold than males. In a major study in which both sexes were encouraged to look at a selection of different humans, the females got bored more quickly than the male dogs in the test.

One, Two, Three o'Clock, Four o'Clock – Snack

How Cats and Dogs Count, Tell the Time and Do Calculus

CATS ARE exceptional timekeepers. They have internal clocks that are so accurate they can be used to time events to within a second.

In one experiment, a group of cats were placed in cages for either five or twenty seconds and rewarded with food treats when they were released. The food would be hidden in one of two feeders depending on the length of time the cat had been in the cage. If a cat had been in the cage for twenty seconds the food would always be in the left-hand feeder; if it had been in the cage for five seconds the food would be in the right-hand one.

Researchers were able to train the cats to pick the correct feeder more than 80 per cent of the time, which indicated the cats knew the difference in the times they were in the cages. They then went on to see if the cats could distinguish between cage times that were much closer in length. Half of the cats were able to distinguish between a five-second stay in the cage and an eight-second stay and therefore choose the correct feeder.

In another test, cats could tell the difference between a sound that lasted four seconds and one that lasted five seconds. They have also been observed deliberately delaying their response to a stimulus by several seconds, down to an accuracy of one second.

Cats are also experts at time management and seem to know when not to waste their time. In tests, a group of cats were trained to repeatedly press a bar to open a tray of food from which they were then free to eat for as long as they liked. To begin with it took forty presses to open the tray, but the number was then increased steadily so that by the end it required more than 2,500 presses of the bar to get a meal. As the experiment progressed, the researchers found that the cats adjusted their behaviour significantly. They began eating fewer meals and eating much more at each meal.

When the researchers varied the number of presses needed to access the food the cats started eating amounts that reflected the number of presses it took to get the food, suggesting they were working out a 'price' for each meal.

DOGS CAN tell the time too. During his famous experiments, Pavlov trained dogs to expect to receive food every half an hour. But when he changed the rules of the experiment and failed to give them anything, they still started salivating after almost exactly thirty minutes. Consciously or unconsciously, their internal clocks had told them to expect food.

Another Russian scientist, V. S. Rusinov, studied the brainwaves of dogs, recording their patterns while the dogs did a variety of tests and training exercises, each one at the same time every day for a period of five days. When Rusinov popped into his lab one weekend, he discovered that the dog who had been tested at that precise time each day the previous week was displaying the same brainwave patterns as he had then. He concluded that the dogs were aware of time and started to think about their tests when their daily time slot arrived.

DOGS CAN count – up to three, at least. In an experiment, researchers showed dogs an edible treat, then raised a screen so that the animal could no longer see it. In full view of the dog, they would then place another treat next to the first, also behind the small screen. When the screen was removed, if there were two treats there (as would be expected) the dog looked only briefly. If, however, there were three treats or one treat (because the experimenter had secretly added or removed one), then it looked for longer. The researchers think that this is because the dogs were expecting two, since 1+1=2, and were surprised when this was not the case.

DOGS KNOW when they're outnumbered. A study of dogs in Italy observed that in a total of thirteen aggressive confrontations between undomesticated dogs, the side with the numerical disadvantage always withdrew before the dispute escalated. This applied whether the smaller number comprised only one dog or a group, which suggests dogs can make judgements about numbers when they find themselves in aggressive situations.

DOGS DO calculus. The discovery was made by a mathematician, Tim Pennings, while he was walking along the beach with his dog Elvis. Pennings noticed

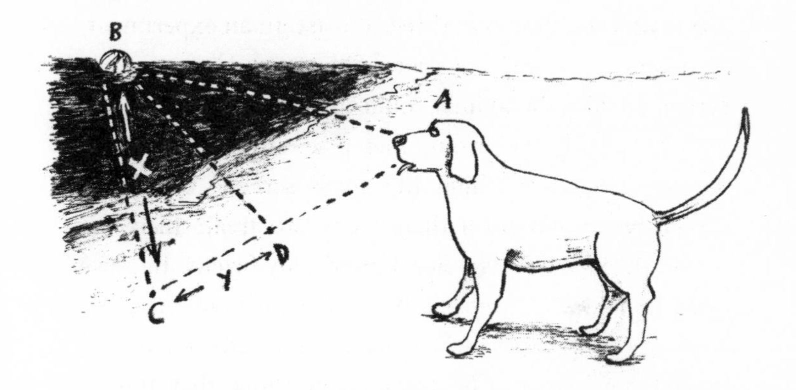

how, when he threw a tennis ball into the sea for Elvis to retrieve, the dog would always carefully work out the optimal path needed to minimize the time it took him to reach the ball.

Sometimes Elvis would run along the beach until he was directly opposite the ball, then swim out to get it. Other times he would plunge into the water right away and swim out to the ball. His most common tactic, however, was to run part of the way along the beach then swim out to reach the ball.

When Pennings analysed Elvis's tactics over a period of time, he found that the dog was behaving in a way that matched a calculus-based mathematical model of the problem.

It read:

$$Y=\frac{X}{\sqrt{r/s+1}\quad\sqrt{r/s+1}}$$

PERHAPS CURIOSITY did kill the cat. Its brain is so active, a cat pumps 20 per cent of its blood supply to it, even though the brain weighs around 7 per cent of its overall body weight.

THE TEN brightest breeds of dog (ranked according to their ability to understand new commands in less than five repetitions and to obey first commands 95 per cent of the time or better) are:

1. Border Collie
2. Poodle
3. German Shepherd
4. Golden Retriever
5. Doberman Pinscher
6. Shetland Sheepdog
7. Labrador Retriever
8. Papillon
9. Rottweiler
10. Australian Cattle Dog

THE TEN least bright breeds of dog (ranked, with most intelligent first, in descending order of ability to understand new commands, even after hundreds of repetitions) are:

1. Basset Hound
2. Mastiff
3. Beagle
4. Pekingese
5. Bloodhound
6. Borzoi
7. Chow Chow
8. Bulldog
9. Basenji
10. Afghan Hound

Cat intelligence rankings

THE TELEVISION station Animal Planet ranked cat breeds according to a sliding scale of intelligence, from three stars, denoting low intelligence, to ten stars, indicating relatively high intelligence. This is how they ranked the best-known breeds:

3 stars	Exotic Shorthair
	Himalayan
4 stars	Persian
5 stars	None

6 stars	American Shorthair
	Birman
	Bombay
7 stars	Abyssinian
	American Curl
	American Wirehair
	British Shorthair
	Cornish Rex
	Cymric
	Maine Coon
	Manx
	Ragdoll
	Scottish Fold
	Snowshoe
	Somali
8 stars	Burmese
	Chartreux
	Devon Rex
	Egyptian Mau
	Japanese Bobtail
	Korat
	Norwegian Forest Cat
	Ocicat

	Russian Blue
	Siberian
	Singapura
	Tonkinese
	Turkish Angora
	Turkish Van
9 stars	Balinese
	Bengal
	Colourpoint Shorthair
	Havana Brown
	Javanese
	Oriental Shorthair
	Siamese
10 stars	Sphynx

One, Two, Three o'Clock, Four o'Clock – Snack

NOT-SO-DUMB MUTTS

Some Other Curious Feats of Canine and Feline Intelligence

DOGS KNOW how to medicate themselves. Canines displaying signs of being unwell have been observed seeking out plants to make themselves vomit. They have returned to normal health soon afterwards.

DOG SALIVA is an effective medicine. It has anti-bacterial properties and is particularly good for stopping wounds becoming infected.

THE CAT'S purr may be a self-healing mechanism. Cats purr at between 25–50 hertz, a frequency at which vibrations have been found to have a wide range of medical benefits, from increasing bone density and helping in the healing of fractures, torn tendons and muscles to generally relieving pain.

Because cats purr not only when they are content, but

also when they are hurt, in distress or giving birth, some scientists think they use purring to heal themselves. They also think it explains why cats rarely suffer bone- or joint-related diseases, including hip dysplasia, arthritis and ligament problems. Purring's healing power may even explain why bone cancers, such as myeloma or osteosarcoma, are almost unheard of in cats. It may also be why respiratory problems are relatively rare in cats. Purring helps to open the airways.

CATS IMPERSONATE snakes. Many creatures mimic other, more dangerous animals in order to protect themselves and scientists think the cat is one of them. To convince predators that it is a dangerous reptile rather than a relatively harmless mammal, the cat has learned both to hiss and to spit like a snake.

Some scientists think that, early in its evolution, the cat even went so far as to imitate the markings of snakes. Tabby cats, who are most closely related to so-called 'ancestral cats', have snake-like markings and, in the wild, sleep coiled up near rocks and tree stumps. This may be to fool birds of prey who look down and see what they imagine to be a snake rather than a cat.

DOGS AND cats frequently display levels of practical

intelligence – or common sense – that confound their owners. A cat in the USA, for instance, dialled 911 when its owner fell out of a wheelchair. Police called to the scene found the man, Gary Rosheisen, lying paralysed on the floor. When they examined the premises they saw that he could not have used either of the special alarms installed in the house. One was above his bed upstairs, while the other was on a necklace, also upstairs, which he had forgotten to wear. The investigators did, however, find his ginger cat Tommy sitting next to the telephone.

CATS CAN raise the alarm in other ways too. A cat in

Cairns, Australia, recognized the danger when a mattress caught fire after a cigarette had been left on it. The smoke failed to set off the house's smoke alarms but the quick-thinking cat worked out what was going on, headed to its master's bedroom and scratched his face to wake him up. The man managed to get himself, his wife and children out before the blaze took hold of the home.

PART FOUR

Is She Really Going Out with Them?

The Truth About Cat and Dog Relationships

JUST LIKE BIRDS, BEES and educated fleas, cats and dogs spend large chunks of their adult lives doing it – or at least trying to. Relationships are never easy, of course. Female dogs, for instance, are much pickier than female cats, which is hardly surprising given the number of clueless suitors the canine world contains. Male cats, on the other hand, don't seem to have a care in the world. Except, that is, when their partners are being unfaithful, which they almost always are. Of course, sex usually carries a price. When all the fun's over, both cats and dogs have to live with the consequences: children.

While the Tomcat's Away, the Wife's at Play

Cats, Dogs and the Mating Game

Cats are highly promiscuous. Male cats, in particular, really aren't fussy about who they mate with. When researchers in France tracked the behaviour of a white tomcat for a year, they found he fathered sixty-three kittens. That's one every six days or so.

Female cats can be nymphomaniacs. Siamese and Persian cats in particular have been observed having unusually high numbers of sexual encounters during oestrus. The condition has been associated with cystic ovaries and brain damage.

TOMCATS REMAIN lotharios even in old age. A twenty-seven-year-old cat was observed in hot-blooded pursuit of a much younger female.

Appropriately enough, the feline world's equivalent of Casanova is an Italian. In the mid 1990s, scientists in Rome studied ten different females, who during the test period produced eighteen litters. Amazingly, 95 per cent of the kittens delivered were fathered by the same male. The researchers were able to be sure of this thanks to the tom's extremely rare coat-colour gene. It was present in virtually all the kittens born to the ten mothers.

SOME FEMALE cats are easier than others. In a study of a community of male and female cats, the group's fifteen females displayed very different mating habits when they were in oestrus, or heat. They were all promiscuous. Six mated with every male that presented himself, while three mated with more than half of the males. Six cats, however, chose to have sex with half or less than half of the males that courted them. The study also revealed that cats can form relatively lasting partnerships. All of the cats tended to have sex with their male partners on more than one occasion and ended up with one male as their preferred partner by the end of the season. No one male was the number one choice of two females.

MALE CATS appear to be possessive and certainly don't like the idea of sharing. Indeed, knowing their partners are being 'unfaithful' makes them less fertile.

Another major study of a large group of cats discovered that when females were in oestrus at different times, the dominant males in the community tended to be given priority by all the receptive females.

However, when females came into season at the same time, the top cats weren't able to stop their harem mating with other, lower-ranked males ahead of them. The impact on the high-ranking males' potency during these seasons was dramatic. They were four times more successful when they had the females to themselves.

FEMALES LIKE older, fatter cats. They also like males who can look after themselves in a fight. Studies of sexual behaviour in large groups suggest age, size and dominant behaviour is a key influence on a female's choice of mate.

FEMALE CATS can reach puberty at any time between three and a half and twelve months of age. Burmese cats tend to have their first oestrus cycle earliest, while Persian cats tend to reach puberty at a more mature age, sometimes as late as eighteen months old.

Male dogs are obsessed with bottoms. Dogs of both sexes greet each other by sniffing. However, a study found that while females tended to concentrate this process on the head area, males tend to pay more attention to the other dog's backside.

Unlike most cats, dogs are extremely choosy about their mates. Female dogs in particular have very strong ideas about what does – and doesn't – make a good-looking male. In an American study, researchers found that some 'good-looking' males were attractive to all females. Other, seemingly less attractive, males, however, were shunned by all females. In fact, females found these 'ugly' dogs so repulsive, they attacked them if they tried to strike up a sexual relationship.

IN COMMUNITIES of wild dogs, the more males that are interested in a female dog, the less likely she is to successfully mate with any of them.

WHEN PUSH comes to shove, however, dogs don't need other dogs to produce puppies. They can also mate with coyotes, wolves and jackals and still produce fertile offspring that are capable of continuing their blood line.

MALE SEXUAL activity drops in autumn in the northern hemisphere. This coincides with the female being unreceptive.

HOMOSEXUALITY IS common in dogs. In studies, males from a variety of breeds have been observed mounting, then stimulating, each other until one or both dogs ejaculate. Among those breeds observed in these same-sex relationships are Beagles, Basenjis, Weimaraners and Cocker Spaniels.

This behaviour may have been inherited from the dog's ancestor the wolf. Within wolf packs only the highest-ranking members mate. When the highest-ranking female is in heat and the sexual temperature is at its peak within the pack, lower-ranking male wolves frequently mount one another. They do this to preserve the pack's pecking order, even though there are lower-ranking females who would be available for sex.

DOGS CAN be bisexual. One leading study of sexual behaviour in animals cited the case of the female leader of a sled-dog pack taking part in a race across Alaska. During the course of the journey, the female had sex with both male and female members of the pack. (Her behaviour was described by the team's human leader in a book about their eventful journey, *My Lead Dog Was a Lesbian.*)

Cats have gay and lesbian affairs too. Females have been observed mounting and stimulating each other's genitals. Males have also been seen bringing each other to orgasm. This too may be rooted in their ancestry. Homosexuality is common in other cats, including lions and cheetahs. In the wild between 27 and 40 per cent of cheetahs live in same-sex relationships.

Heavy Petting

Some Truths About Cat and Dog Sex

CAT SEX lasts for between one and four minutes. Experienced males can complete the process in 1.8 minutes on average. The ejaculation part of the process takes an average of eight seconds.

ONE MAJOR study of the sexual activity of male cats found some were capable of having sex ten times in an hour. The average frequency of sex in the twelve toms observed in the study was 5.8 times an hour.

A pair of cats have been observed mating eight times in twenty minutes.

DESPITE THEIR insatiable appetite, however, cats do indulge in what you might call heavy petting. Males and females conduct elaborate courtship behaviour, including grooming each other, lying side by side and rubbing each other. What's more, this foreplay is repeated between each copulation.

DOG SEX can, by contrast, go on for hours. Intercourse happens when the bulbourethral gland on the male's penis swells inside the female, stimulating her vulva to contract around it and prevent it from withdrawing. Ejaculation starts after between fifteen and thirty seconds and can continue for half an hour or more, although the sperm will have been transmitted within the first two minutes or so.

Scientists think this is nature's way of flushing through the semen. Every thirty seconds or so the male will release fluid to flush the semen further into the female. 'Ties' can go on for long periods. Some breeders have watched their dogs hooked up together for three and a half hours.

When the tie is finally broken, both male and female will vigorously groom their genital areas to rid themselves of any harmful bacteria.

CANINE SEX is a tricky business and requires practice for a male to become proficient. A mere one in fifteen males successfully achieves a tie during the first year of its life. Some fail to get it right in almost forty attempts.

SEX IS a noisy business in the feline world. Female cats have a special cry to alert males to the fact they are receptive to sex. The so-called 'heat cry' is a monotonous howling and can last up to three minutes.

The male cat's penis is equipped with spikes. The screeching, ear-splitting noise the female makes at the end of sex is in part a cry of pain as it is withdrawn. Females can also lash out aggressively at their male partners as they withdraw. Despite this, mating behaviour can start all over again minutes later.

Dogs experience orgasms. Scientists who attached cardiotachometers to dogs during sex noticed significant rises in their blood pressure. The dogs' reactions were very similar to those of humans, who experience rising heart rates during sex. The scientists think the dogs were experiencing climaxes like humans.

Male dogs can suffer psychological trauma after being neutered. (In the 1990s, an enterprising American firm began producing plastic testicles, or 'Neuticles', that replaced the removed real ones. Predictably, when their product proved a hit with vets and dog owners, they proclaimed they were 'the dog's bollocks'.)

Male tortoiseshell and calico cats are almost always sterile. This is because they have an extra X – or female – chromosome. (Most tortoiseshell and calico cats are female.) As a result, these males very rarely show any interest in females. Other cats often treat these cats like kittens.

Stray dogs commit rape. Studies of packs of feral dogs have observed powerful males forcing themselves on inexperienced females.

UNSURPRISINGLY, CATS suffer from sexually transmitted diseases. The cat form of HIV is feline immunodeficiency virus, or FIV. Cats don't get it from actually having sex. Instead, it is transmitted through saliva when male cats bite females hard on the neck while they are copulating. Males can get FIV from bites they receive during fights with other males. Curiously, the cat's cousin the cheetah also gets FIV, but doesn't become ill as a result. No one has yet explained why.

SOME TOMCATS get so frustrated that they will mount males who are in the process of mounting females.

MALE CATS and dogs masturbate. Both tend to do so with inanimate objects like fluffy toys or slippers. Female cats with high oestrogen levels masturbate. They tend to rub their genital area against the floor while licking it at the same time.

IN LABORATORY tests, tomcats have willingly had sex with artificial vaginas.

WHELP!

How Cats and Dogs Cope with Birth and Beyond

FEMALE CATS can conceive from sex with several males during the same heat cycle, so most litters have more than one father. As a result, it's relatively rare that kittens in a litter are full brothers or full sisters, even though they are born at the same time.

DOGS HAVE false pregnancies. Females will display all the symptoms of being expectant, including lactating and putting on weight, but fail to produce puppies.

CATS ACT as midwives. Scientists have observed female cats helping out with deliveries. The midwife cat will lick clean the kittens as they emerge and clean the perineum of the cat giving birth. The cat will also eat the amniotic membrane, the lining surrounding the kitten when it is born.

THREE IN ten new-born puppies die for no apparent reason, a phenomenon known as Fading Puppy Syndrome.

A FEMALE cat in labour can deliver kittens once every thirty seconds or so. It can, however, take as long as fifty minutes between each delivery.

An average mother cat has between one and eight kittens per litter, though a litter may contain as many as thirteen kittens. In one case a cat was discovered to be carrying eighteen foetuses.

One cat was recorded as having 420 kittens over a period of seventeen years. The oldest known mother was pregnant at the age of twenty-six.

Cat's milk contains eight times more protein and three times as much fat as human milk.

Kittens double their birth weight within a week of being born. Within two weeks they have trebled it and within three weeks they will be quadruple their birth weight. Males and females grow at roughly the same rate until the age of eight weeks, when males start to grow faster.

For the first two to three weeks of their lives neither puppies nor kittens can go to the toilet on their own. Instead, their mothers stimulate their abdomen and perineal regions so that they urinate and defecate as a reflex response. The mothers then lick up or eat whatever their children have produced.

In packs of feral dogs, other females, particularly those who have had false pregnancies, will produce milk and share wet-nursing duties with new mothers.

Male cats are sometimes child-killers. Scientists in France, studying a population of free-ranging domestic cats, were disturbed to observe six cases of infanticide, where strange males entered nests and killed the kittens. Infanticide may be one of the reasons why mother cats move their nests frequently. They keep on the go to avoid being found.

PART FIVE

Eats Goats and Leaves

Canine and Feline Food and Drink

GIVEN THEIR DEEPLY DISSIMILAR backgrounds, it's hardly surprising that canine and feline eating habits are so different. Cats tend to prefer opportunistic snacks to large meals. Dogs, on the other hand, are generally, like us, fond of a healthy three meals a day. (There are exceptions, though: given a choice, Beagles, Poodles and Basenjis prefer to snack like cats.)

Canines are also more adventurous than cats when it comes to food. While cats turn their noses up at sweets and other treats, dogs will eat almost anything. The down side of this, however, is that their devil-may-care attitude gets them into trouble. Which is what drug-taking cats get into as well . . .

Cats Snack, Dogs Have Dinner

Why Both Are What Their Ancestors Ate

OLD EATING habits die hard. Scientists think that canine and feline eating patterns are related to those of their ancient ancestors.

In the wild, the domestic cat's distant relative would eat regular light meals, mainly small birds and rodents. As a result of this, the cat evolved a body and metabolism that are set up to eat little and often. This is why owners find their cats pining for meals so often. The intervals we humans have between breakfast, lunch and supper seem like an eternity to cats.

Dogs, on the other hand, have evolved feeding patterns that are much more like ours. In the wild, their ancestors hunted large prey, working as members of a co-operative pack. They then sat around together sharing a large and often lengthy feast. As a result they are more comfortable eating larger meals less often.

DOGS HAVE forty-two teeth. Cats have only thirty. The make-up of their mouths reflects their very different dietary habits. At the front of the mouth, both have six incisors and two canines, used primarily for ripping. At the back of the mouth, however, dogs have more molars and premolars. These are used chiefly for crushing plants, roots, vegetables and bone, which cats don't eat.

CATS ARE experts at plucking feathers. When they capture a bird they quickly strip it of its plumage to get to the skin underneath. For some reason, however, American and European cats have completely different techniques for plucking. European cats move their heads in a zigzag fashion as they withdraw a feather from a bird's skin. American cats draw the feathers out with one, long vertical movement. No one has yet explained why this is.

DOGS HAVE more taste-buds than cats. They have around 1,700, almost four times as many as cats, which have approximately 470.

WHILE, IN general, canines are what scientists call neophilic, willing to try new things, cats are the opposite, neophobic, much less keen on trying new things.

A CAT'S tastes are moulded when it is a kitten. During weaning its mother gives it a set of food preferences which remains in place for the rest of its life.

From then on a cat is extremely fussy about eating anything that it hasn't tried before. So, despite the fact that raw meat is closer to the diet it would have in the wild, a domesticated cat raised on tinned cat food will shun uncooked cuts of meat that don't look and smell like the processed product. Farm cats are less fussy, because they're used to eating raw food from an early age.

Cats don't eat exactly the same thing all their life, however. Researchers have found that if cats are offered a type of food that they haven't had for a while, they show a very strong preference for it over their regular diet. It's been suggested that this might help them to eat a nutritionally balanced diet, because they take in vitamins and nutrients that they may recently have been lacking.

The cat's picky nature doesn't always work to its advantage. Because of their specialized diet, cats don't have the same kind of metabolism as other animals and aren't able to break down certain compounds. This means that in a lot of cases they can't, for instance, metabolize drugs. Medicines that can cure other animals of many ailments are toxic to cats.

Cats are hypercarnivores. This means they need a much higher amount protein in their diet than almost any other mammal. An adult cat needs its diet to contain 12 per cent protein while a kitten needs half as much again, 18 per cent. Dogs are capable of living healthily on much less than this. An adult dog needs a diet of only 4 per cent protein. This is why dogs

are much better suited than cats to vegetarian diets.

As a result, cats' taste-buds are tuned in to the taste of fish, birds and other creatures. They react to amino acids that are found in flesh and tend to reject any foods that don't contain them.

DOGS IN the wild, on the other hand, eat a diet that is 80 per cent meat. They supplement this with plants and fruits. So, while they strongly favour meat tastes, they also react to a sweet-tasting chemical called furaneol which is present in many fruits and especially tomatoes. The 'sweet tooth' that the modern dog has evolved as a result of its ancestry gets it into a lot of trouble, however.

Chocolate, for instance, can be poisonous to a dog because it contains high levels of theobromine, which is a cardiac stimulant and diuretic. Cocoa powder and cooking chocolate are particularly bad for canines. A 10 kilogram dog can become seriously ill by eating half of a 250 gram block of cooking chocolate. It may experience nausea, palpitations and even a heart attack. Dogs can die of chocolate poisoning.

RAISINS AND grapes can also be fatal to dogs. Vets have reported cases of severe kidney failure in dogs that have eaten large amounts of raisins or grapes. In one study of dogs treated for the problem, half the dogs were found to have died from the effects of renal failure.

Cats don't like sweet things, mainly because they can't taste them. By analysing the cat's genetic code, scientists learned that part of the code that normally provides an animal with sweet-taste receptors is missing. This has left cats simply unable to detect sweet-tasting compounds such as sugars and carbohydrates.

Unlike humans, both dogs and cats can taste water. A dog's ability to do this can actually increase, according to how much salt it has eaten. The more salt a dog has eaten, the more sensitive the taste-buds are to water, and so the tastier it seems. The receptors are in the tip of the tongue, which is used for lapping.

The average dog takes in just over a litre of water a day. It gets half of this from drinking water and half from ingesting food. On average a dog drinks nine times a day.

Cats have highly efficient kidneys, which protect them from dehydration and allow them to get by on small amounts of water.

This is why cats that largely eat tinned food – which can be as much as 83 per cent water – drink water only very occasionally. Scientists think this is an echo of their past as desert-dwelling animals. A cat that has been dehydrated by 6 per cent takes twenty-four hours to rehydrate. (By contrast, a dog does so in an hour.)

SOME CATS drink with their paws rather than their tongues. Researchers have observed them dipping their paws into water, then sucking the moisture out. Scientists think it is a genetic trait.

DURING HOT weather, it is not unusual for a dog's food consumption to decrease. Studies show that, as a general rule, dogs need about 7.5 per cent fewer calories with each ten-degree rise in temperature.

BITCHES ARE much more prone to obesity than males. Middle-aged dogs are twice as likely as younger dogs to be overweight.

PUPPIES EAT much less when they dine alone. Studies have found that puppies eat up to 50 per cent more food if they eat with their litter mates.

CATS ARE much less likely to become overweight than dogs. One vet reported that 30 per cent of dogs that came to his clinic were overweight. Only 10 per cent of cats suffered from obesity.

Anorexia, however, is more common in cats than dogs, though dogs can suffer from it. In their case, the condition is often associated with anxiety about being separated from their owners.

DOGS ON diets fight less. In a study of small dogs put on calorie-restricted diets to combat obesity, the number of aggressive situations they on average found themselves in dropped from one every eight hours or so to zero.

DOGS EAT faeces – and not just canine ones. They are particularly fond of cats' droppings, which are high in protein because of the feline diet, and horse manure, which is also high in nutrition. Eating faeces – or coprophagy – is most common in small dogs and those that don't get much exercise.

CATS AND DOGS can get cravings to eat the most bizarre things. This need to eat non-food items is known as pica and can involve dogs consuming anything from linoleum to electrical cords, coins and clothing to kitchen knives.

In the case of cats, usually it is fabric – particularly wool – that is consumed. Scientists think the condition is the result of factors such as stress, obsessive-compulsive disorders and brain damage. It can also be caused by sheer hunger.

DOGS CAN become seriously ill and even die if they eat or drink a range of things found in most ordinary homes. These include cigarette tobacco, alcohol, mothballs, pot-pourri oils, dishwasher tablets and ground coffee.

Many common garden plants and flowers are also poisonous to dogs. They include privet, wisteria, azalea, yew, ivy, daffodils and clematis. Dogs can also be poisoned by rhubarb leaves and tomato vines.

Dogs also poison themselves by drinking antifreeze. This contains a sweet-tasting chemical called ethylene glycol, which is a powerful stimulant to the dog's sweet taste-buds. When dogs find pools of antifreeze that has leaked from radiators on to roads or garage floors they lap it up greedily, often with serious consequences. Small amounts of antifreeze can cause 'drunkenness', vomiting, depression and diarrhoea. A significant amount will result in death by poisoning.

Onions, garlic and macadamia nuts are all poisonous to dogs.

Pet food is driving cat evolution. Scientists think that domestic and feral cats may be evolving to become genetically different from each other more quickly now than they have in the whole history of domestication. Because cats need to take in a diverse range of vitamins and nutrients, they have in the past usually had to hunt for birds and rodents to achieve a balanced diet. Now, however, pet foods are available that contain everything a cat needs, so there is less of a requirement to hunt. This means, researchers have suggested, that there is no longer selection for domestic cats to be able to hunt, and as a result they are becoming genetically more distant from feral cats.

DOGS PRODUCE different types of saliva. Some are very watery, while others are richer in mucus. Scientists think the salivas perform different functions. The mucus, for instance, is better at breaking down meat, while the watery saliva is more suited to digesting vegetables.

THE WHIFF of food on someone else's breath may seem pretty repulsive to us. To dogs, however, it's irresistible. In tests, unfed dogs that had just interacted with fed dogs had a strong preference for foods that they had got a whiff of on the other dogs' breath.

CONTRARY TO the familiar saying, old dogs can learn new tricks – provided, that is, they are following a healthy lifestyle. A study discovered that when elderly Beagles were fed on a diet of fruit, vegetables and vitamins and exercised regularly they were able to learn a whole range of new tasks. Scientists think the healthy regime and mental stimulation stave off the onset of Alzheimer's and other brain-related illnesses common in older dogs.

BLACK CATS don't eat jelly. If they did they'd be reddish-brown. Scientists think a cat's colour may be dependent on what it eats. They discovered that black cats that ate a lot of gelatin turned a russet-brown colour.

Kangaroo and Tortoise Eggs

What Cats and Dogs Eat in the Wild

DOGS PREY on a variety of animals around the world. On the Cayman Islands they eat snakes. In Australia their main target is sheep and, to a lesser extent, cattle. Dingoes sometimes also attack kangaroos. It's thought that dogs wiped out two species of wallaby in New Guinea. In the Galapagos, dogs prey on iguanas, penguins, pelicans and sea-lions. The island's real delicacy, as far as dogs are concerned, however, is tortoise eggs.

THE KAKAPO, a large, flightless New Zealand parrot, is almost extinct largely because of feral cats preying on their numbers. Cats have also been blamed for the disappearance of two other bird species, diving petrels and broad-billed prions on Herekopare Island.

AUSTRALIAN CATS love possum. When a study was carried out in northeast Victoria, remains of the common ringtail possum were present in 56 per cent of cats' droppings.

WHEN DOMESTIC cats and dogs were introduced to the Turks and Caicos Islands they quickly wiped out

the indigenous population of iguanas. Within two years all 15,000 had been killed by the two species.

ENVIRONMENTALISTS IN Australia blame cats for killing some of the country's most endangered species. In the Australian states of Victoria and New South Wales alone, the local population of 900,000 domestic cats were reckoned to kill around 60 million creatures a year, with each cat eating on average eight birds a year. Australia's 3.8 million feral cats kill a similar number of animals a year. Endangered species now facing extinction because of cat predation include the rabbit, golden bandicoot and the burrowing bettong. Curfews and restrictions on the number of cats a household can keep have been introduced as a result.

AN AMERICAN study of more than two hundred cats found they each caught and killed between ten and fifty animals a year. Their captures included mice, rats, frogs, other reptiles, goldfish and forty-seven types of bird. The study also showed how subtle cats are at hunting. Cats with bells on their collars caught just as many animals as those without. As a result of this, 50 to 60 per cent of cats in the United States are not allowed out at night.

Cats are molecatchers. They use their exceptional hearing abilities to catch moles as they burrow their way to the earth's surface. Just as the mole begins to emerge, the cat will scratch it out of the ground. This is a rare example of cats taking the offensive in the hunt. Their most successful tactic is to sit, wait and pounce. Cats rarely eat moles, however.

Cats can fish. As well as hunting rodents and birds, cats catch fish swimming in lakes, ponds and rivers. To land their catches, they use a cunning 'flip' technique. Depending on the size of their prey, they will dip one or two front paws into the water and quickly slide them under the fish's belly. They will then flip the fish out of the water, throwing it behind them, over their heads, on to land, where they will eat it. A Dutch study observed cats using this technique to catch fish much bigger than themselves.

When kittens throw a ball up into the air as if to catch it, they are not playing. In fact they are practising the fishing techniques they would use if they were living in the wild.

The most skilled angler is the Sri Lankan 'fishing cat' (*Prionailurus virverrinus*). It dives head first into swamps and lakes to catch its prey.

TOM AND Jerry aren't always natural enemies. In fact, given a choice of other animals to eat, cats sometimes avoid hunting and killing mice altogether.

A study of feral cats living on islands around the world where they and mammals weren't originally natives found that their first choice of food was rabbit. If rabbits weren't available, rats were their preferred meals. While mice were a common part of cats' diets in temperate regions, on tropical islands like the Galapagos, Jarvis and Frigate Island it was very rare, if ever, that a cat ate a mouse. No one has yet explained why.

THE SPANISH introduced aggressive Bull Mastiffs to the Pacific island of Juan Fernandez in 1686 specifically to control the goat population, an important source of food for mariners in the region. Unfortunately they had not counted on the dogs flourishing there. By 1830 the Bull Mastiff population had grown so big it was a danger to the humans on the island. The dogs were exterminated.

Cats are vampire hunters. A study by Argentine scientists found that cats living on cattle farms targeted by blood-sucking bats successfully attacked the predators on a regular basis. The cats were so good at catching the bats that they significantly reduced the number of cattle bitten by the vampires.

Cannibalism is common in cats, especially in colonies of feral felines. Often it is mothers who eat aborted foetuses and still-born kittens. Scientists think they do so for sanitary reasons and also to prevent predators from being attracted to the den. If she is extremely underfed, a mother may even kill and consume a kitten so as to give herself the nutrition she needs to care for the rest of the litter. Stress, particularly over where to raise the litter, can also lead a mother to eat her new-born. In a colony, other females may also kill and consume kittens.

Rex and Drugs

How Cats and Dogs Get High

Cats can become addicted to hallucinogenic drugs. Their number-one narcotic is catnip, a mint-like plant that contains an oil called hepetalactone. Not all cats are sensitive to hepetalactone, but those that are experience a hallucinogenic reaction that sends them on a 'trip'. A 'tripping' cat can display a wide range of strange symptoms, from rolling on its side, to twitching and leaping in the air animatedly.

In Japan, cats get high on the matatabi plant, which also contains a hallucinatory oil. Cats that have been affected by matatabi have been seen lying on their backs with their legs in the air.

Addiction can run in the genes. A cat's reaction to catnip is largely inherited from its parents. A kitten with only one parent sensitive to the drug has a fifty–fifty chance of developing the sensitivity when it reaches maturity. A kitten with both parents sensitive has at least a 75 per cent chance of growing sensitive to it.

Catnip doesn't usually do any long-lasting damage to the cat. A trip generally lasts for around ten minutes. Afterwards the cat returns to its normal, 'sober' state. Prolonged use of the drug, however, can leave cats chronically 'spaced out' and unaware of their surroundings.

CATNIP AND matatabi are not the only plants to have this property. Cat thyme and valerian have the same effect. However, if cats are given catnip or valerian internally they act as tranquillizers, or 'downers', rather than uppers. No one has yet successfully explained why this is.

DOGS GET high on cannabis. Vets have reported cases of pets having accidentally ingested their owners' supplies of marijuana. In one a cross Collie bitch that had swallowed a 2-gram chunk of cannabis resin became clumsy and uncoordinated. It also became obsessed with staring at its reflection in a shiny metal dustbin. Another dog, a Staffordshire Bull Terrier bitch, ran around the

room snapping at thin air after 'passively' breathing in a joint.

DOGS ARE addictive to humans. One study found that 54 per cent of dog owners admitted they were hooked on their pets in the way a smoker, alcoholic or junkie is reliant on their drug.

PART SIX

How Lassie Comes Home and Tom Always Lands on His Feet

Cats and Dogs in Motion

LIKE EVERY OTHER CREATURE, cats and dogs need to get from A to B and – if at all possible – back to A again. With threats lurking behind every corner, they also need to be able to take flight, sometimes literally. So both have evolved their own, unique ways of doing the locomotion. Dogs are masters of speed and endurance, while cats are highly skilled gymnasts, capable of squeezing through any gaps and flying through the air like a cross between a parachutist and an ice-skater. For reasons that no one can quite yet agree on, they are also both capable of epic journeys using navigational skills that would put Christopher Columbus to shame.

Making Tracks

How Cats and Dogs Put One Paw in Front of Another

Puppies take their first tentative steps at around twelve days of age. They learn to move backwards before going forwards.

All cats are digitigrade. This means they walk on their toes. Their weight is distributed across the balls of their feet by their soft toe pads.

The cat has a symmetrical walk, with its left limbs moving in sequence together, half a stride apart from its right limbs. The giraffe and the camel are thought to be among the few other animals that walk this way.

Cats normally walk at around 0.9 metres a second. That's just over 3 kilometres or 2 miles per hour. They are able to perform a speedy walk, or amble, at twice this speed, however.

As they move through the gears to go faster, cats rely on their forelimbs much more than their back, or pelvic, limbs. When running at full speed their back limbs hardly touch the ground at all. A cat in full flight is – almost literally – flying. At maximum speed, a cat's front limbs spend only around 20 per cent of the time in contact with the ground.

Most breeds of domestic cat can reach speeds of up to 30 miles per hour. The Egyptian Mau, exceptionally fast, can reach up to 36 miles per hour.

WALKING BACKWARDS is an awkward-looking process for cats. To do so they have to perform an extreme bend of their spine, something other animals, including dogs, don't need to do. Scientists think the reason for this lies somewhere in their evolutionary past, although they haven't worked out where yet.

SOME 84 per cent of dogs go for a run when they are let off the leash.

GALLOPING DOGS breathe at the same rate they run – that is to say, one breath per stride.

BECAUSE OF their lack of large numbers of sweat glands, dogs use panting as their main means of cooling off. Since dogs can't sniff and pant at the same time, a sniffer dog's ability to do its job is drastically reduced if it has been running hard.

DOGS PANT 200 times a minute. Cats pant 250 times in the same period.

SCIENTISTS HAVE discovered that a dog refrigerates its brain during exercise, allowing it to stay cool no matter how energetically it runs around. At rest, a dog's brain is maintained at a higher temperature than the blood supply pumped to it from the heart. But when it starts running around and the blood supply temperature starts rising, the brain stays cool, around 1.3 degrees centigrade lower. Scientists have identified a mechanism – or cartoid rete – in the arteries at the base of the brain. As warm blood pumps up from the heart the rete protects the brain from overheating by pumping cool blood from the nose and mouth.

Young puppies can't shiver. Adult dogs use shivering to generate heat but puppies don't learn to control their body temperature until they are three weeks old.

Cats instinctively react to cold by baring their teeth and walking around in circles.

Greyhounds can reach speeds of just under 40 miles per hour.

Sled dogs are marathon champions among land mammals. They are the fastest of all mammals over distances of ten miles and more, able to lope along at an average 20 miles per hour for more than an hour. Sled dogs can easily cover more than 100 miles a day, day after day.

Racing sled dogs are most active around sunrise and sunset.

OFFERED A ride on a fire engine or a horse-drawn carriage, Dalmatians automatically assume a safe position underneath the vehicle's chassis. A study of this behaviour concluded it is a genetic habit instilled in the breed from their past. Centuries ago Dalmatians were popular companions for firemen and coach drivers.

DOGS ARE capable of mastering many alternative forms of transport. They have been observed water-skiing, surfing, riding horses and motorcycles and balancing on the top of fast-moving pick-up trucks.

They Fly Through the Air with the Greatest of Ease

How Cats and Dogs Defy Gravity

In 1987 two vets, Wayne Whitney and Cheryl Mehlhaff, at the Animal Medical Center in New York, conducted a five-month study of cats brought in for treatment after accidentally falling from the windows of Manhattan skyscrapers. The cats had fallen from between two and thirty-two storeys (25 and 400 feet) and had almost always landed on concrete pavements below. In total Whitney and Mehlhaff treated 115 cats, with an average fall of just over five storeys (75 feet). Of these only three cats were dead on arrival at the clinic, while a further eight failed to recover from their injuries within the next twenty-four hours. Amazingly, 104 of the 115 cats – just over 90 per cent – survived. By contrast, a human's chances of surviving a fall of four storeys (50 feet or so) is reckoned to be no better than fifty–fifty. Their chances of surviving a six-storey fall on to concrete are virtually nil.

The most remarkable survivor in the Whitney/ Mehlhaff study was a cat called Sabrina. She fell thirty-two storeys (400 feet) on to the pavement below and emerged with nothing more than a mild chest injury and a chipped tooth.

CATS THAT fall from higher altitudes have a better chance of survival. Of cats that fell from between seven and thirty-two storeys only 5 per cent died. By contrast, 10 per cent of the cats that fell from between two and six storeys suffered fatal injuries.

The cat owes its amazing ability to survive falls from huge heights – the so-called High-Rise Syndrome – to a combination of three factors.

First, cats don't fall through the air as fast as heavier, denser animals such as humans. A cat reaches a maximum falling speed, or terminal velocity, of 60 miles per hour within 100 feet.

Secondly, a cat uses a brilliant self-righting system that,

regardless of the direction its body is pointing when it starts the fall, repositions its feet so that they are pointing downwards within moments. Cats achieve this by using the vestibular system inside the inner ear. This is in effect an internal gyroscope that transmits three-dimensional information about the direction of gravity, linear motion and the orientation of the head. Within 70 milliseconds of falling, a cat's brain has received signals telling it to extend its legs ready for landing. If the head isn't aligned to face downwards the neck muscles rotate it into place. Once this self-righting mechanism has positioned the body properly the cat is free to relax and spread its limbs out horizontally, like a flying squirrel, to reduce its velocity.

Last but not least, cats are able to land with their limbs flexed so as to dissipate through the soft tissue in their legs the impact of hitting the ground. They effectively do the same as parachutists who are trained to land with their knees and hips flexed to prevent injury.

Scientists think the ability to fall without injury is rooted in the cat's ancestry and its links with the African wild cat. As a tree-dwelling animal, it evolved techniques for falling successfully from great heights.

FOR MANY years the cat's self-righting ability baffled scientists, who couldn't work out how it turned its body in mid-air when it had nothing to push against. In theory every swivel of the body should produce a corresponding swivel in the opposite direction, which should mean the cat lands all twisted up. A French doctor, Étienne Jules Marey, solved the puzzle by filming a cat falling, then slowing the recording down to sixty frames a second. He saw that the cat performs a two-part manoeuvre.

First the cat turns its forequarters towards the ground, then swivels its hindquarters in the same direction. Marey saw that by changing the position of its paws between the two phases the cat uses its front and rear to counteract each other. This is the same principle as an ice-skater controlling a pirouette by drawing in the arms close for fast spins and extending them for slower turns. The cat does both moves simultaneously: it draws in its forepaws and thrusts out its hindpaws. That way it is able quickly to make a half-turn of its forequarters towards the ground while its rear end turns only a little in the opposite direction owing to the resistance created by extending its hindpaws. To bring its hindquarters around, the cat reverses the procedure, thrusting out its forepaws and drawing in its hindpaws. Even cats with missing tails or limbs are able to do this.

Subsequent to this discovery, other scientists have

concluded that cats use their eyes to orient themselves as they fall through the air.

Cats are so good at landing on their feet that damaged jaws and nosebleeds are much more common than damaged legs or backs.

Cats are born with the ability to right themselves. Studies have revealed that kittens know how to right themselves from their backs to an upright position nine days before birth. They know how to fall safely as soon as they are born, three weeks before they learn to walk. They learn to self-right themselves in mid-air from the age of four weeks.

Small dogs that fall from buildings are prone to more serious injuries than cats.

Dogs can parachute too – well, sort of. One of the most remarkable recipients of the British Armed Forces animal equivalent of the Victoria Cross, the Dickin Medal, was a dog called Rob.

A canine member of a parachute regiment who took part in twenty missions behind enemy lines during the Second World War, he would parachute down with his human colleagues, then watch over them while they slept between their undercover operations. He took part in successful missions in north Africa and Italy.

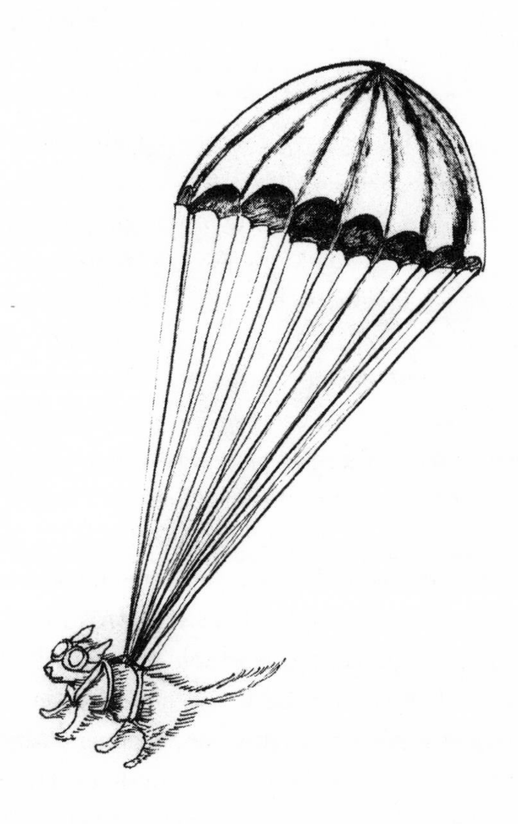

THE LASSIE PRINCIPLE

How Cats and Dogs Usually Find Their Way Home

LONG BEFORE Disney made *The Incredible Journey*, scientists were researching the phenomenal homing abilities of cats and dogs.

In 1922 *Science* magazine reported on a one-year-old Collie whose owners moved 160 miles, from Canon City to Denver, Colorado. Within a week the dog was back at his old home, having crossed the Arkansas River and a mountain range, including the giant Pike's Peak.

In 1994, it was reported that a blind Cocker Spaniel called Sadie safely returned close to home after losing her owner 45 miles away.

CATS FREQUENTLY track down owners who have moved home without them.

In France, a tabby called Mimine spent thirteen months trying to find her family, who had moved 500 miles from Toulouse in the south to Treveray in the north, leaving Mimine seemingly happily settled into life with another family. But to their amazement the cat turned up over a year later. They immediately recognized her by the distinctive way she rubbed and caressed the family's two young daughters. In another case a cat travelled 2,300 miles across the breadth of the United States, from New York to California, to be reunited with its family there.

IN SOME instances, cats seem to sense families are moving home before they have even done so. When a family from Louisiana returned from Texas, where they had been looking for a new home, they discovered their pet Beau Cat was missing. Five months later, when they had moved to Texas, Beau Cat appeared in the playground of the school at which the mother of the family had begun teaching.

AN AMERICAN scientist, Francis Herrick, conducted one of the earliest and most extensive tests of the homing instinct of cats after trying to re-home a kitten that had grown up in a barn at his home in Cleveland, Ohio.

Herrick had taken it on a tram to its new owner on the other side of the city 4½ away. Despite the fact it had never been away from home before, the young cat reappeared on his doorstep within a day and a half, having crossed through the heart of the city and negotiated a railway bridge and a 400-foot climb on the way.

Intrigued by this, Herrick repeated the experiment with a mature female with kittens that were about to be weaned. He took the cat away on seven different occasions. Each time the cat returned within three days at the most. It was taken up to 3 miles away, in a different direction each time. To be sure it couldn't see where it was going the cat was blindfolded on one occasion. Another time it was anaesthetized for the journey. It still made it back.

CATS DEFINITELY have an excellent sense of direction. In a much-publicized experiment conducted in Kiel, Germany, a group of cats were taken on a circuitous journey miles from their homes, then released into a giant maze that had been set up in a field. The maze, which was covered so that the cats could not use the sun as a guide, was arranged like a clock and had openings every 15 degrees. The cats were free to do as they pleased. Most immediately exited the maze, leaving through the opening that was pointing most accurately to the direction in which their homes lay.

SOME SCIENTISTS believe cats are so sensitive to the earth's magnetic field that they can navigate by it. An American team repeated the Kiel experiment with similar results. But the researchers also discovered that the cats' homing abilities were reduced significantly if they had magnets attached to their collars. They also saw that older cats fared better than younger cats. This too supported the magnetic theory because as cats age more metal is naturally deposited in their brain.

Intriguingly, in the American maze experiments the cats performed less well when they were tested more than 7½ miles from home.

Some scientists think dogs use their sense of smell to guide them home. On encountering familiar odours from other dogs they have been in contact with and whose 'home range' overlaps with theirs, they employ this information to calculate the right direction in which to head.

There is no shortage of controversial theories to explain cats' and dogs' remarkable homing instincts.

The maverick Rupert Sheldrake argues both are guided back to their owners by the 'morphic fields' that bind humans and their pets psychologically as well as physically. His argument is an extension of his explanation for why dogs know when their owners are coming home.

There is, however, an even more radical explanation. According to some, cats and dogs are exhibiting another extrasensory ability, this time called 'psi trailing'. The idea behind this is based on atomic physics, and the theory that all electrons function in pairs, with one spinning in the opposite direction to the other. When one changes direction, the other senses this and changes its direction, too. A specialist in parapsychology, Dr Myrna Milani, has suggested that there may be such a strong bond between pets and their owners that separation creates a disequilibrium at the atomic level. This can only be corrected by them being reunited. The scientific community is yet to take the idea very seriously.

DOGS THAT roam or run away are much more likely to be male and un-neutered. One study discovered that 94 per cent of dogs with a history of running away stopped doing so when they were castrated. Scientists think the males are simply heading off in search of sexual encounters.

DOGS DON'T always arrive home safely, unfortunately. Studies by vets have shown that 87 per cent of the trauma cases they see are dogs that have been run over by cars as they tried to walk on or cross roads. One in eight dogs dies from its injuries.

Cats, by contrast, benefit not only from their ability to find their way home but also their gift for making near miraculous recoveries from serious accidents. In a University of Cambridge study of 127 cats involved in serious road accidents, 93 survived, 58 of them with moderate to very severe injuries. They stayed in hospital, on average, five days and took just twenty-three days' treatment to recover.

Fat Cats Can't Jump

Why Some Cats and Dogs Don't Get Around So Well

CATS GET stuck up trees because of an evolutionary design fault. Their claws curve under, making them a useful tool for climbing upwards but not so handy when climbing downwards, as they can't grip so effectively then. As a result cats tend to use a far-from-graceful backwards sliding technique to dismount trees. If that fails, they call the fire brigade.

FAT, STUBBY cats can't jump. A study of the physiology of a group of eighteen cats revealed that the best jumpers had longer hind legs and a lower body-fat mass. These cats were able to generate the greatest amount of all-important TOV, or takeoff velocity. Cats with more body-fat mass and shorter legs generated less TOV and, in extreme cases, could barely get off the ground.

DOGS AREN'T always in control of their movements. They have a reflex action rather like the human knee jerk. If a dog's flank is touched briefly and lightly, its hind paw rises up to scratch the flank as a reflex. The dog has no control over this action.

DOGS ARE born with an equivalent of a thumb on the side of their feet. The extra digit, known as the dew claw, is a remnant of their evolutionary past that has become obsolete. The dew claw can be a handicap for working dogs in particular, as it can get caught in undergrowth and bushes.

ELDERLY DOGS aren't so good at finding home. Those that suffer from the dog equivalent of Alzheimer's disease – known as Canine Cognitive Dysfunction – become increasingly confused and forget much of what they have learned in early life, including where they live. If they get lost they are unlikely to find their way back.

CATS DON'T have collar bones. This isn't a handicap at all, though. The lack allows them to get in and out of any hole no smaller than the size of their head.

PART SEVEN

The Cat Pack

The Social Lives of Cats and Dogs

NO CAT OR DOG is an island (except for the Maltese, possibly). Both species have to share their world with other cats, dogs and humans, as well as assorted other creatures. This brings its own challenges, of course. Cats and dogs face family strife, political power struggles and, worst of all, confrontations that demand they fight their corner. For many of them, though, they can at least be sure of the protection of their best friend in the world: you and me.

12.4 CHILDREN

The Family Life of Cats and Dogs

TOMCATS HAVE a bad reputation as parents and are commonly portrayed as absent fathers. But one study of farm cats discovered that, far from being feckless, toms were active in family life. Researchers observed the males helping the females to defend their kittens from other, invading males. They even found that, when the mothers were absent, the males protected any abandoned kittens. The toms made the litter feel secure by curling themselves around the new-borns.

Sometimes, they even help to suckle and bring up the kittens of others in their colony, carrying them to new nest sites if the group 'moves house'.

Siamese dads take more interest in their kittens than do fathers in other breeds. New Siamese fathers will lie with their offspring and groom them.

Cat mothers teach their young how to kill their prey. Mothers start the learning process by bringing dead prey to their litter. As they learn how to eat the prey the kittens progress to lessons with living prey. The mother supervises as the kittens learn to catch, kill and – if necessary – recapture prey if it escapes. Studies have shown that kittens who have to learn these lessons without their mothers present are less efficient hunters when they reach maturity at around six months of age.

Kittens know their mothers really do know best. In one study, scientists discovered that kittens learned much more quickly from their mother than from a stranger. The kittens that watched their mother pushing a lever to obtain food picked up the technique much more quickly than kittens that watched a stranger performing the same thing.

Young dogs and cats learn not to kill their friends. Dogs that grow up on farms surrounded by chickens, for instance, don't attack the birds that are familiar to them.

One scientist's husky lived happily alongside a group of five chickens, but when the five grew old and two new ones were introduced the dog killed and ate both newcomers. The five old chickens remained untouched.

Similarly, cats don't display their predatory instincts to animals they grow up with or get to know. One scientist conducted a study in which he fed a daily diet of rats to a wild golden cat. One of the rats managed to evade the cat and hid under its bed. The cat got used to it being there and became friends with it. The cat continued to eat every new rat that it was given. But its friend was left in peace for the four months before it was

removed. When the rat was returned three months later, the cat had forgotten it, however. It ate it then.

Scientists think this is because both animals develop their predatory hunting skills after the so-called 'critical' learning period during which they concentrate on social development. In all these cases, the cats and dogs concerned had learned to treat their 'friends' differently.

Dogs don't forget their mother. Studies have found that puppies can still recognize their mother even after two years of separation. The strong feelings are mutual: mothers can recognize their offspring after spending a similar period apart.

The bond between siblings is not so tight, however. When separated, brothers and sisters forget each other and don't recognize one another if they are reunited.

Wild dogs make better fathers. Studies have shown that feral dogs play an active role in the care of their offspring. They help with chores, from grooming and playing with the puppies to retrieving them when they try to escape from the den before time. This behaviour is much rarer in domestic dogs.

12.4 Children

DOGS MAKE natural foster parents. Scientists think that the instincts of the wolf pack, in which all female members share child-rearing duties, remain embedded in domestic dogs. As a result, females are often relaxed about taking in another female's offspring and caring for them.

Leaders of the Pack

How Cats, Dogs and Other Animals Live Together

Feral dogs form gangs. Typically these gangs are made up of ten members: two males and eight females. The leader is always a large male. He forms the pack by barking loudly until he has enough members. The gang sticks together for between one and two and a half weeks on average.

Leadership within a feral gang is tested regularly. The leader asserts his dominance at feeding times and while they are travelling. To ensure his rule is obeyed, the feral gang leader can attack and kill weaker members without any warning.

DOMESTIC DOGS that are allowed to roam free from home also team up in groups. They form small gangs of between two and five dogs. Strays do this too. They will tend to move over larger areas than the free-ranging dogs and will avoid humans more often. Stray packs will also tend to stick together longer than other gangs of dogs.

CATS ARE far from the solitary creatures they are commonly thought to be. Given the choice, cats will congregate in groups, but the size and structure of their communities will depend on one crucial factor: food. Studies have shown that cats will live in groups if there is sufficient food. If food supplies are too widely dispersed to support a colony, however, they will fend for themselves and live alone.

IN COLONIES, cats greet each other by touching noses.

CATS DISPLAY authority in non-violent ways. Some higher-ranking cats tend to groom lower-ranking cats, for instance. The groomers adopt a higher posture, standing or sitting upright while they groom the other cat, which tends to sit or lie down. They generally groom the head and neck area, as if confirming their superiority.

Scientists think grooming is a way of redirecting potential aggression in groups of cats.

Grooming calms cats down. They will often lick themselves after an aggressive situation. They also groom themselves when they think a storm is brewing.

Cats signal aggression by lashing their tail from side to side.

It's a woman's world – at least, if you are a cat. Studies of feline colonies have shown they are strongly matriarchal in nature – that is, females are the dominant sex socially. The hierarchy is headed by a queen, her adult female offspring and her extended family.

Cats make friends and enemies. Members of cat colonies form strong associations with other members. These friends groom, greet, rub and sleep next to each other. However, there are other members of the community with whom cats don't form strong bonds. Males are more likely than females to have these enemies, which are also more likely to be male.

Female cats are freer spirits. In wild groups of cats,

females are more likely to leave the group and head off to lead an independent life.

CATS CAN be bullies and thieves. A major study of a colony of cats saw that some members intimidated and stole from others, particularly those they saw as close to them in social rank. The mugger moggies would move through the group, threatening and taking items that they didn't even need in a clear attempt to impose their authority over others. The scientists behind the study think poor early socialization may produce these anti-social cats.

CATS AND dogs can also form strange partnerships with other species. Both have been known, for instance, to adopt injured birds. A cat in the city of Porto Alegre, Brazil, was reported to have raised a bird it discovered lying on the floor, unable to fly after falling from its nest. The cat and the bird, normally predator and prey, shared the same eating bowl. The bird even adopted the cat's meat-rich diet. Most extraordinarily of all, the bird allowed itself to be used by the cat as bait so that it could trap – and eat – other birds.

In similar fashion, a Chihuahua in China adopted an orphaned chick. The dog acted as the chick's surrogate

parent, watching over it and picking it up in its mouth and taking it safely home when it risked getting into trouble.

DOGS WILL allow the offspring of other species to suckle from them. A kitten and a pair of tiger cubs have been observed feeding off the breast of dogs in China.

A DOG and a giant black bear have been observed by scientists happily cohabiting in the captive bear's cage.

CATS ARE not intimidated by bigger animals. Jack, an American family tabby, achieved fame in June 2006 when he chased a huge black bear up a tree. When the bear gingerly came down, Jack chased it up another one.

CATS AND dogs don't necessarily fight all the time. Cats are more likely to be chased if they are running away from a dog. The sight of the fleeing cat triggers a dog's deep-rooted instinct to carry out prey-chasing. Cats learn to avoid being hurt by a chasing dog by lying down and freezing, with their body and head flattened to the ground. Denied the thrill of the chase, the dog will often lose interest.

Dog breeds that have been trained to work with livestock, such as the Border Collie and Welsh Corgi, are much more likely to chase and bark at a cat, especially if it is on the move. They are, however, less likely to progress to attacking a cat, as their training requires them simply to guide rather than hurt their 'prey'.

Bosom Buddies

How Cats and Dogs Evolved into Man's Best Friends

Dogs are more closely related to sea-lions than they are to cats. Geneticists have traced the ancestry of both animals back to the period around 40–50 million years ago when modern carnivores emerged from two 'superfamilies', known as Canoidea and Feloidea.

The Canoidea clan evolved into a wide range of species, from canines like the dog, jackal and Arctic fox to such diverse mammals as the skunk, giant panda and the walrus.

The hyena, curiously, belongs to the same superfamily as cats. So does the mongoose.

The most recent DNA studies have confirmed that the domestic dog evolved from the wolf. Scientists are divided on when this happened, however. Some argue it occurred 100,000 years ago; others claim that it was a far more recent development, closer to 15,000 years ago. On one thing most are agreed, however. The dog almost certainly evolved in the Far East, probably in China. Geneticists think the dog is closest in its make-up to the Chinese wolf.

A grave in Ein Mallaha in Israel dating back 12,000 years to 10,000 BC contained the skeleton of a woman cradling a puppy.

The earliest archaeological evidence of dogs in Europe was found in Star Carr in Yorkshire. The dog bones found there date back to beyond 7,000 BC.

The widespread belief is that wolves evolved into dogs once they were accepted into human society. Some researchers, however, argue that the change happened while the wolf was living as man's neighbour rather than his domestic companion. According to this theory, wolves would never have had the right temperament to live with humans but some were bold enough to start living off the scraps of food ancient villagers discarded. The wolves that were confident enough to live in close proximity to humans like this thrived, evolving so as to be more and more compatible with their new neighbours. Those wolves that were wary of the strangers, however, grew apart, remaining essentially the same creature that we see in the wild today.

By contrast, cats may have been natural companions for humans. One major study of the cat family found that friendly behaviour towards humans is common throughout the cat family. It concluded that it's likely cats were domesticated because they were already on good terms with humans. Their ability to control vermin made them even more attractive as housemates.

Cats also originated in Asia, but quickly spread around the globe into Europe and Africa and across the Bering land bridge joining Russia and Alaska to reach North America. They then crossed the Panamanian land bridge to reach South America.

All thirty-eight members of the modern cat family are believed to be descended from just eight ancestors: the ocelot, panther, caracal, baycat, Asian leopard, puma, lynx and the domestic cat. The domestic cat evolved from the African wild cat and six species of small cats that thrived around the Mediterranean.

The earliest evidence of cats living with humans was discovered in Cyprus. The bones of a cat were reckoned to date back to 6,000 BC. Scientists think that at this point humans were capturing and taming cats rather than breeding and domesticating them.

Dogs – of some kind – are found on all but one of the earth's continents, Antarctica.

According to one study, all 701 modern breeds of dog evolved from ten superbreeds that emerged from the Far East. These ten 'progenitor' breeds were bred selectively to fulfil specific tasks. Sight hounds, specialists in coursing game and ancestors of the modern greyhound and Afghan Hounds, emerged in Mesopotamia around 4,000 to 5,000 BC. Scent hounds, forefathers of the Bloodhound, Foxhound and Dachshund, appeared around 3,000 BC. Working and guard dogs probably emerged in Tibet around 3,000 BC, paving the way for descendants such as the Rottweiler, the Saint Bernard and the Bulldog. Toy and companion breeds, the ancestors of breeds like the Poodle and the Pug, emerged at around the same time. For reasons that haven't yet been explained fully, they came from Malta.

AMERICAN BREEDS of dog are descended from European, not American, wolves. Scientists think that when Europeans crossed the Bering Straits to colonize the Americas 10,000 to 15,000 years ago, dogs were by their side. These first settlers seem to have discouraged the breeding of native American dogs.

THE FIRST domesticated cats are believed to have been kept in Egypt. The earliest depictions of cats there date from the third millennium BC. A cat wearing a collar is depicted in the tomb of Ti, dating from around 2,600 BC. In tombs dating back to 1,900 BC a group of seventeen cats were found buried with small pots of milk.

THE EGYPTIANS revered both cats and dogs. When a cat died of natural causes the occupants of its home all shaved their eyebrows. When a dog died they shaved their whole bodies, including their heads.

The export of cats was illegal. The Egyptians sent agents to Mediterranean ports to buy and repatriate cats that had been smuggled abroad. This is believed to be

one of the reasons why cats appeared in Europe relatively late compared with dogs.

IN 50 BC, the historian Diodorus Siculus wrote of a Roman soldier who killed a cat while in Egypt and was lynched on the spot by an angry mob.

SOME RESEARCHERS think that the Egyptians bred cats specifically for the purpose of sacrificing them.

THE ANCIENT Libyans worshipped the cat as a god. Between 950 and 880 BC, residents of the then capital Bubastis were gripped by a cat cult, building temples to the feline goddess Bastet or Bast.

THE GREEKS loved their dogs but weren't so keen on cats. Aristotle described the female cat as 'a particularly lecherous animal that actively wheedles the males on to a sexual congress'.

THE ROMANS weren't much taken by cats either. The Greeks introduced them to Rome in the fifth century BC, but they were not popular. It was not until nine hundred years later, when Palladium discovered they were useful for catching moles in artichoke beds, that they became widespread. Until then ferrets were more popular.

THE ROMANS produced the first 'Beware of the Dog' signs. Notices warning '*cave canem*' were found in Rome and Pompeii. The signs were intended to protect the dogs rather than the citizens, however. Historians think they were designed to warn people against stepping on the small Italian Greyhounds that were popular at the time.

The Romans were also the first to use dogs as guide dogs. On the wall of a house buried in ash during the famous eruption of Vesuvius at Pompeii is a depiction of a blind man with a staff being led by a small dog, dating from 74 BC.

You could call them bosom buddies. Dogs were so successfully integrated into human society in South America that human mothers often acted as wet nurses for orphaned puppies. They provided milk for the first four weeks until weaning began.

Cats only moved to the Americas in the seventeenth century. Early settlers had them imported to deal with an invasion of rats.

Wild dingoes are actually descendants of domestic dogs. Researchers think their ancestors arrived in Australia on trading boats with their human owners around 4,000 BC. At this point they were probably sources of food, which is why some of them escaped into the outback, where they evolved into wild dingoes.

By contrast, the Polynesian dog, or kuri, arrived in New Zealand with the Maori when they settled there. It happily adjusted to domestic life on the islands, even though the Maori regarded kuri as a delicacy and ate them on a regular basis.

Soul Mates

Why Cats, Dogs and Humans Are Made for Each Other

Dogs are much better at understanding humans than supposedly more intelligent – and closely related – animals. In one major study, for example, even very young puppies performed much better than chimpanzees at reading human communication signals. Asked to pick 'blind' one of two containers of food, one of which was empty and one full, they were able to spot signals and clues humans gave them to make the right choice. While dogs were alert enough to spot looks and gestures so as to choose the right bowl nine times out of eleven, chimpanzees got it right only twice in eleven attempts. Scientists think that this gift for understanding humans was one of the main reasons ancient man chose to domesticate the dog in the first place.

DOGS ALSO know when – and when not – to beg. In an experiment involving dogs and chimps, both animals were given the choice of begging from someone who could see them or someone who could not. The chimps failed to appreciate that there was little point in begging from a human with a bucket over his head. The dogs, on the other hand, knew not to bother begging from a person who had his back turned to them.

DOGS, IT seems, are highly tuned to their master's voice. And they don't perform well to versions that aren't the real thing.

In a test carried out at de Montfort University, a group of dogs trained to respond to the 'sit' and 'come' commands performed less well when a tape recording of their trainer's voice was played. Dogs also like to make eye contact with those who are training them. In the test, the dogs responded badly to the 'sit' command when the trainer turned her back on them.

IN SOME ways, it's no surprise dogs and humans understand each other so well. Poodles and humans, for instance, share 75 per cent of the same DNA.

Both dogs and cats can follow human pointing gestures. When researchers presented them with two bowls and pointed to the one that contained hidden food, both dogs and cats chose the right bowl significantly more often than chance expectations. Some scientists think that dogs, at least, understand to some extent the communicative meaning of pointing. It's possible that understanding human 'body language' has developed as dogs became more domesticated. Wolves, although they can learn to follow pointing, take much longer to do so than dogs, even when reared under identical conditions.

Dogs rely more on humans for help than cats do. An experiment found that dogs presented with an unsolvable problem look at their owner for help. Scientists gave dogs bowls of food that they couldn't get to, and found that they soon stopped trying and started looking at their owner, then looking back at the food, then back at the owner. Interestingly, they didn't look at the other humans that were present in the room. Cats, on the other hand, ignored everyone and carried on trying to solve the problem themselves, adding credence to the idea that they are more self-sufficient.

Cats and humans have very similar neurological systems. As a result, scientists have used studies of the way the feline brain works to better understand the human mind. Cats, for instance, have provided useful evidence on how, when and why strokes occur in humans.

Scientists have found that cats not only suffer dementia when they get older, they can also develop Alzheimer's disease.

Cats also led scientists to isolating a natural brain chemical that triggers deep sleep. A study revealed the presence of high levels of a chemical called adenosine when cats were deprived of sleep for longer than usual. Scientists think this could lead to the development of better drugs to help people with insomnia or other sleep problems.

A dog's brain is also very similar to that of a human. Maps of human and canine brains reveal that they both control vision from an area at the back of the brain, hearing from the side, near the temples, and touch and control of movements from a narrow band running across the top of the brain.

Dogs and humans are the only animals with prostates. Dogs suffer from prostate problems too.

CATS AND dogs are good for human health. The idea that our pets may help prevent illness and even reduce heart disease was first raised in the 1980s when researcher Erica Friedmann at the University of Maryland found that recovering heart-attack patients tended to live longer if they had cats or dogs. A 1991 study at Cambridge University then discovered that, within a month of acquiring a cat or dog, people suffered less from headaches, backache and flu. In 1992, an Australian study at the Baker Medical Research Institute in Prahran found that, out of a sample of 5,741 people attending a heart clinic, the 784 patients who owned pets had an average cholesterol level that was 2 per cent lower than those who didn't. This was reckoned by epidemiologists to lower their risk of a heart attack by 4 per cent.

NUMEROUS SCIENTIFIC studies have proved that having dogs or cats around significantly lowers stress and blood-pressure levels. Feelings of depression and loneliness, too, are lessened by having a feline or canine companion. In one study of long-term residents of a nursing home, for instance, researchers discovered residents felt less lonely after spending time alone with a dog than they did after spending time with a human visitor accompanied by a dog.

Dogs improve people's social lives. In one extensive study of dogs and their owners, scientists found that a woman experienced three times as many conversations with strangers when she took a dog with her on a walk than when she did the same thing alone. When a male subject was used, the effect was even greater. He experienced ten times as many conversations as normal.

Dogs bring out the maternal instincts in women. An Italian study found that being in the company of dogs evoked different responses in men and women. Females, for instance, talked to the dogs much more than males. Intriguingly, they also talked in an affectionate, simplistic, mothering language, as if they were talking to a child.

A study in 1995 found dog owners were 8.6 times more likely still to be alive one year after a heart attack than those who did not own a dog.

One study claimed that dogs have a more positive influence on health than cats do. As with previous studies, it claimed that dog owners had lower blood pressure and cholesterol, fewer minor physical ailments and were less likely to have more serious medical problems. Unlike previous studies, however, this study suggested the effects were greater with a dog than a cat.

OPINION IS wildly divided on whether cats and dogs are always good for children. One study at the Keck School of Medicine of the University of Southern California suggested that having a dog in the home may worsen asthmatic children's response to air pollution. In a study of 475 children with asthma, those with dogs had significantly increased cough, phlegm production and bronchitis when they were introduced to measured pollutants, including nitrogen dioxide, ozone, particulate matter and acid vapour. There were no increases of these symptoms in children who lived in homes without pets or who lived with cats but no dogs.

OTHERS THINK that living with cats increases young children's risks of getting eczema. In a study of 134 children with cats at home, 27.6 per cent had eczema by the age of one year, compared with 17.8 per cent in a sample of 286 households without cats.

SOME THINK the opposite is true, however. In an Australian study, children in households with a cat or dog were 30 per cent less likely to suffer from nausea, diarrhoea and vomiting.

And in another study, children who lived with two or more dogs or cats during their first year of life were found significantly less likely to develop allergies in later years. The finding was cited as evidence of why children who live in a house with a pet tend to spend more time at school. Yet another survey found that five- to eight-year-olds received, on average, nine days more schooling a year if they owned a pet.

Cats and dogs in the main live happily within human society. There are times, however, when the three species don't get on.

A large number of studies have identified specific patterns to dog attacks on humans. The dogs that are most inclined to bite are young, male adults. Frequently they are members of large breeds and haven't been castrated. Often the dogs know the victim. The most likely victims are boys under the age of ten.

In 1991, the US Centers for Disease Control and Prevention analysed the data on 178 dog bites reported in the city of Denver, Colorado, that year. Dogs that fell into the category 'male, un-neutered, under five years of age or weighing more than 20 kilograms' were significantly more likely to bite. Dogs that were chained in yards were also more likely to bite. Among breeds, German Shepherds and Chow Chow were the most likely, Golden Retrievers and Standard Poodles the least likely to bite.

DO DOGS suffer from the Curse of the Werewolfhound? According to the *British Medical Journal*, there are around 200,000 incidents of dogs biting humans each year in the UK. But, if one study is to be believed, the number of attacks increases significantly when there is a full moon.

An analysis of patients admitted to Bradford Royal Infirmary with dog bites revealed that the number of cases increased sharply when the moon was full and fell away equally steeply when it began to wane again.

Intriguingly, however, an Australian study found no correlation between the lunar cycle and dog bites.

DOMESTIC CATS are as likely to attack their owner as they are another cat. Cases of cats being aggressive towards humans made up just under one sixth (or 16.1 per cent) of cases reported to the UK's Association of Pet Behaviour Counsellors in 1997. Incidents involving cats being aggressive to other cats was almost identical: 16.8 per cent.

PART EIGHT

Dr Labradoodle

How Cats and Dogs Have Become Breeds Apart

EVER SINCE OUR ANCIENT ancestors began selectively breeding dogs to fight, guard their sheep and keep them company at night, we have become ever more obsessed with moulding them to suit our whims. Today there are hundreds of individual breeds, from the tiny Chihuahua to the gargantuan Great Dane, from hairless Sphynxes to Persian fluffballs. Predictably this has produced animals that are different in ways that go significantly beyond their mere appearance. But this has also come at a price.

Cats Aren't From Mars

Some Odd Truths About Cat and Dog Breeds

The Romans were dog lovers and became the first society to breed selectively. They developed fighting, herding, guard and lapdog breeds.

The basic construction of a dog's skeleton is the same, regardless of whether it is a Pekingese or a Saint Bernard. The skeleton of a wolf is identical too.

Cats and dogs have similar numbers of vertebrae. The only exception is the Manx cat, which is well known for being tail-less. This birth defect is caused by a dominant gene that Manx kittens inherit from one of their parents. If a kitten is unlucky enough to inherit the same gene from both mother and father it will not survive to birth.

Dogs that look like wolves behave like them. A study by a team of behavioural scientsts at the University of Southampton looked at the social behaviour of ten different breeds, comparing them with their ancient ancestor the wolf. They chose fifteen typical wolf behaviours, from aggression to submission, and recorded how many of them were displayed by the dogs.

Intriguingly, the breeds that behaved most like wolves were the ones that looked most like them. The Siberian Husky, the most wolf-like of the tested dogs, displayed the most mature range of wolf-like behaviours.

Some breeds don't grow up. The same University of Southampton study found that, while some breeds displayed behaviour similar to that of adult wolves, others, particularly 'toy' breeds, behaved like wolf cubs all their lives. The most juvenile-looking breed, the Cavalier King Charles Spaniel, displayed only two threat behaviours: growling and physically displacing a rival. In the wild, this conduct is limited to wolf cubs under twenty days old.

Some scientists think this is no accident and that man selected and bred dogs with more 'juvenile' personalities (a process called paedomorphosis). They picked these animals deliberately because they were better suited to life in human society.

ONE OF the most popular breeds of cat in the world today is the Ragdoll, a large but highly docile and friendly feline. The breed was developed in the 1960s by an eccentric Californian, Ann Baker, who claimed the cat had a rather extraordinary background. According to Baker, the cat was a mixture of feline, human, skunk and extraterrestrial and had been developed with the help of a secret US Government agency. Baker held that the Ragdoll was the missing link between humans and aliens. The truth, however, was less dramatic. Far from being from Mars, the Ragdoll was from the Middle and Far East. It is a cross between a female Persian Angora and a male Birman whose kittens had then been bred with Burmese cats.

PET DOGS are worse at dealing with problems than working breeds. A comparative study carried out in Hungary found that dogs in a companionship relationship with humans performed significantly worse in a simple task than those who have a working relationship with humans.

Feline personalities fall into three categories, according to one major study of the species. While the first type is bold, confident, sociable and easygoing, the second is the complete opposite: timid, shy, unfriendly and nervous. The third type of cat is active and potentially aggressive.

Different dog breeds have different personalities. The first major study of these diverse personalities was carried out in the 1980s by a couple, Benjamin and Lynette Hart, of the University of California, Davis. Their study rated different breeds according to certain characteristics, from excitability to aggression, to playfulness and affection-seeking. Below are the breeds that figured at the top and bottom of their rankings in some of the categories.

Most active dogs

Highest-ranking breeds: Silky Terrier, Chihuahua, Miniature Schnauzer, Fox Terrier, Irish Setter, West Highland White Terrier

Lowest-ranking breeds: Basset Hound, Bloodhound, Bulldog, Newfoundland, Collie, Saint Bernard

Dogs most likely to be guilty of excessive barking
Highest-ranking breeds: Yorkshire Terrier, Cairn Terrier, Miniature Schnauzer, West Highland White Terrier, Fox Terrier, Beagle

Lowest-ranking breeds: Bloodhound, Golden Retriever, Newfoundland, Akita, Rottweiler, Chesapeake Bay Retriever

Dogs most likely to snap at children
Highest-ranking breeds: Scottish Terrier, Miniature Schnauzer, West Highland White Terrier, Chow Chow, Yorkshire Terrier, Pomeranian

Lowest-ranking breeds: Golden Retriever, Labrador Retriever, Newfoundland, Bloodhound, Basset Hound, Collie

Dogs most likely to engage in destructive behaviour
Highest-ranking breeds: West Highland White Terrier, Irish Setter, Airedale Terrier, German Shepherd, Siberian Husky, Fox Terrier

Lowest-ranking breeds: Bloodhound, Bulldog, Pekingese, Golden Retriever, Newfoundland, Akita

Dogs most likely to demand affection
Highest-ranking breeds: Lhasa Apso, Boston Terrier, English Springer Spaniel, Cocker Spaniel, Toy Poodle, Miniature Poodle

Lowest-ranking breeds: Chow Chow, Akita, Bloodhound, Rottweiler, Basset Hound, Collie

The Encyclopedia of Cats, written by the well-known vet Dr Bruce Fogle, categorizes cats according to different personality traits, including those that are gregarious or self-contained, sedate or active, quiet or vocal. Here is how some well-known breeds are categorized.

Gregarious cats

Maine Coon, Turkish Angora, Somali, Tiffanie, Balinese, Angora, Oriental Longhair, La Perm, Japanese Bobtail, Havana Brown, Abyssinian, Spotted Mist, Korat, Bombay, Asian Smokes, American Burmese, European Burmese, Tonkinese, Siamese, Oriental Shorthair, Cornish Rex, Devon Rex, Sphynx, Egyptian Mau, Ocicat, American Bobtail

Self-contained cats

Longhair, Colourpoint Longhair, Birman, Ragdoll, Norwegian Forest Cat, Siberian Forest Cat, American Curl, Scottish Fold, Selkirk Rex, Turkish Van, Nebelung, Chantilly Tiffany, Exotic Shorthair, British Shorthair, Manx, American Shorthair, Snowshoe, European Shorthair, Chartreux, Russian Shorthair, Singapura, Bengal, Pixiebob

Sedate cats

Longhair, Colourpoint Longhair, Birman, Ragdoll, Maine Coon, Scottish Fold, American Curl, Selkirk Rex, Cymric, Nebelung, Exotic Shorthair, British Shorthair, Manx, European Shorthair, Chartreux, Russian Shorthair, Singapura, American Burmese, European Burmese

Active cats

Siberian Forest Cat, Turkish Van, Turkish Angora, Somali, Munchkin, Chantilly Tiffany, Tiffanie, Balinese, Angora, Oriental Longhair, La Perm, Japanese Bobtail, American Wirehair, Snowshoe, Havana Brown, Abyssinian, Spotted Mist, Korat, Bombay, Asian Smokes, Tonkinese, Siamese, Oriental Shorthair, Cornish Rex, Devon Rex, Sphynx, Egyptian Mau, Ocicat, American Bobtail, Pixiebob

Quiet cats

Longhair, Colourpoint Longhair, Ragdoll, Norwegian Forest Cat, Scottish Fold, Selkirk Rex, Cymric, Nebelung, La Perm, Exotic Shorthair, British Shorthair, Manx, American Shorthair, American Wirehair, European Shorthair, Chartreux, Russian Shorthair, Havana Brown, Abyssinian, Singapura, Bengal

Vocal cats

Maine Coon, Turkish Angora, Balinese, Munchkin, Angora, Oriental Longhair, Japanese Bobtail, Snowshoe, Spotted Mist, Siamese, Oriental Shorthair, Cornish Rex, Devon Rex, Ocicat

Some Pets Get All the Bad Luck

Breeds That Draw the Genetic Short Straw

In our quest to produce pets of a consistent size, shape and personality, we have drawn on a small genetic pool. In doing so we have also increased the likelihood of puppies inheriting diseases associated with dangerous genes within the breed's DNA. As a consequence, many breeds are prone to a range of serious conditions from cancer to heart disease, skin disorders to bone defects.

A major study by the American Kennel Club concluded that a century of selective breeding had resulted in 25 per cent of pedigree dogs having at least one genetic disorder.

Of the 170 breeds of dog registered with the UK Kennel Club in 1994, only twenty-eight had no known genetic disease or defect. An eye disease, PRA, or Progressive Retinal Atrophy, was one of the most common. Briards, a herding dog from France, were the worst afflicted. Some 30 per cent of them were affected by PRA after reaching the age of eighteen months.

NO WONDER so many dogs are called Spot. Many breeds are prone to acne. Dogs with short coats, such as Boxers, Bulldogs and Doberman Pinschers, are most susceptible. As with humans, spots normally appear on the face, specifically on the chin.

SOME 30 per cent of Dalmatians and 14 per cent of Setters are born deaf in one or both ears, according to a study by Texas A&M University.

HALF OF ROTTWEILERS and Miniature Schnauzers are short-sighted. So too are German Shepherds, a breed that has been developed to work as a guide dog. An American study that looked at a group of dogs bred specifically to be guide dogs found 15 per cent of them were short-sighted.

AMONG DOMESTIC breeds of cat, the Bengal has an unusual affinity for water. It frequently jumps into its owner's bath, generally uninvited.

DALMATIANS GET a kind of gout. Uniquely among dogs they lack an enzyme called uricase, which breaks down uric acid. As a result the acid can build up in joints and cause kidney stones. Dogs that eat lots of red meat containing a substance called purine are particularly prone. As with humans, middle-aged males are most likely to suffer the illness.

Dogs suffer from the only known contagious cancer. The cancer – known as Canine Transmissible Venereal Tumour (CTVT) – spreads through close contact such as sex, licking or biting. Scientists think the cancer originated from a single wolf that lived somewhere between 250 and 1,000 years ago.

Cats get asthma. Only around one in two hundred cats suffers from the condition, with Oriental breeds such as the Siamese and cats aged between one and five most likely to develop it.

Humans are believed to be the main cause of the illness. Cats develop respiratory problems because of household dust, litter and even human dandruff.

Cats also get asthma as a result of passive smoking. Studies have shown that cats who live with smokers also double their risk of getting the feline equivalent of the cancer non-Hodgkin's lymphoma.

Dogs can develop strange, obsessional habits. One study discovered that some breeds are prone to certain traits more than others. German Shepherds, for instance, tend to chase their tails, while Bull Terriers can spend 80 per cent of their waking life spinning round in circles. Doberman Pinschers suck their flanks, while Rottweilers

dig for vermin. The most unpleasant habit, however, is probably the Schnauzer's obsession with constantly checking its anus.

FERAL DOGS are less prone to infectious diseases than domestic ones. Since they live in closed communities, similar to wolf packs, they are exposed to very few outside canines. So even though they live a scavenging lifestyle, often foraging for food in rubbish dumps, they are exposed to far fewer infectious diseases than domestic dogs are.

Other medical conditions common in particular breeds include:

Congenital heart defects
Basset Hound, Beagle, Bichon Frisé, Boxer, Bull Terrier, Chihuahua, Chow Chow, Cocker Spaniel, Collies, Doberman, English Bulldog, English Springer Spaniel, German Shepherd, Golden Retriever, Great Dane, Labrador Retriever, Maltese, Pomeranian, Poodles, Rottweiler, Samoyed, Schnauzers, Weimaraner, Welsh Corgis, West Highland White Terrier, Yorkshire Terrier

Cherry eye (protruding third eyelid)
Beagle, Bloodhound, Boxer, Bulldog, Cocker Spaniel, Lhasa Apso, Shar-Pei

Skin and stomach allergies
Akita, Boxer, Bull Terrier, Dalmatian, English Setter, Golden Retriever, Labrador Retriever, Shar-Pei, Staffordshire Bull Terrier, West Highland White Terrier

Obesity
Basset Hound, Beagle, Cairn Terrier, Cavalier King Charles Spaniel, Dachshund, Labrador Retriever, Rough Collie, Shetland Sheepdog

Cleft palate

Beagle, Boston Terrier, Bulldog, Cocker Spaniel, Miniature Schnauzer, Pekingese

Bloat

Doberman, Gordon Setter, Great Dane, Irish Setter, Irish Wolfhound, Standard Poodle, Weimaraner

Bone cancer

Bernese Mountain Dog, Great Dane, Irish Wolfhound, Newfoundland, Pyrenean Mountain Dog, Rottweiler

Skin diseases

Chow Chow, Miniature Poodle, Pomeranian, Samoyed, Toy Poodle

Acne

Boxer, Bulldog, Bull Mastiff, Doberman, German Short-Haired Pointer, Great Dane

Baldness

Boston Terrier, Chihuahua, Dachshund, Italian Greyhound, Whippet

Alopecia

Bernese Mountain Dog, Dachshund, Doberman, Chihuahua, Chow Chow, Irish Setter, Italian Greyhound, Miniature Pinscher, Standard Poodle, Weimaraner, Whippet, Yorkshire Terrier

Hip or elbow dysplasia

Bernese Mountain Dog, Chow Chow, German Shepherd, Golden Retriever, Labrador Retriever, Newfoundland, Rottweiler, Shar-Pei

Dogs that resemble wolves live longer. While there are exceptions to this rule, the shape of a dog's face is generally a strong indicator of its likely lifespan. The sharper and more wolf-like its face is, the more likely the dog is to live a relatively long life. The flatter the face, the shorter the life.

The most authoritative study of canine lifespans in the UK was published in 1999 by the *Veterinary Record*, the magazine of the British Veterinary Association. The study revealed some surprising facts. For instance, mongrels tend to live longer than most pedigree dogs; only 8 per cent of dogs live beyond the age of fifteen; and 64 per cent die or are put to sleep because of illness. Cancer is responsible for 16 per cent of deaths, twice as much as heart disease. While some terrier breeds live for an average of thirteen or fourteen years, breeds like the Irish Wolfhound may live for less than half this time, often as little as six years.

The study also compiled a list of the average lifespan of the most popular breeds:

Afghan Hound (12.0)
Airedale Terrier (11.2)
Basset Hound (12.8)
Beagle (13.3)
Bearded Collie (12.3)
Bedlington Terrier (14.3)
Bernese Mountain Dog (7.0)
Border Collie (13.0)
Border Terrier (13.8)
Boxer (10.4)
Bull Terrier (12.9)
Bulldog (6.7)
Bull Mastiff (8.6)
Cairn Terrier (13.2)
Cavalier King Charles Spaniel (10.7)
Chihuahua (13.0)
Chow Chow (13.5)
Cocker Spaniel (12.5)
Collie (13.0)

Corgi (11.3)
Dachshund (12.2)
Dalmatian (13.0)
Doberman Pinscher (9.8)
English Cocker Spaniel (11.8)
English Setter (11.2)
English Springer Spaniel (13.0)
English Toy Spaniel (10.1)
Flat-Coated Retriever (9.5)
German Shepherd (10.3)
German Shorthaired Pointer (12.3)
Golden Retriever (12.0)
Gordon Setter (11.3)
Great Dane (8.4)
Greyhound (13.2)
Irish Red and White Setter (12.9)
Irish Setter (11.8)
Irish Wolfhound (6.2)
Jack Russell Terrier (13.6)
Labrador Retriever (12.6)
Lurcher (12.6)
Miniature Dachshund (14.4)
Miniature Poodle (14.8)
Norfolk Terrier (10.0)
Old English Sheepdog (11.8)

Pekingese (13.3)
Multiple-breed/Mongrel(13.2)
Rhodesian Ridgeback (9.1)
Rottweiler (9.8)
Rough Collie (12.2)
Samoyed (11.0)
Scottish Deerhound (9.5)
Scottish Terrier (12.0)
Shetland Sheepdog (13.3)
Shih Tzu (13.4)
Staffordshire Bull Terrier (10.0)
Standard Poodle (12.0)
Tibetan Terrier (14.3)
Toy Poodle (14.4)
Viszla (12.5)
Weimaraner (10.0)
Welsh Springer Spaniel (11.5)
West Highland White Terrier (12.8)
Whippet (14.3)
Wire Fox Terrier (13.0)
Yorkshire Terrier (12.8)

THE OLDEST dog on record was an Australian cattle dog called Bluey. He was put to sleep at the age of twenty-nine years and five months.

The oldest recorded cat was a female tabby that lived to be thirty-four.

Cat breeders have attempted to produce tame household cats that look like wild cats. One attempt to do this was the crossing of the wild Bengal cat with more conventional domestic breeds. The result was a striped cat that resembled a toy tiger. Naturally it was christened the Toyger.

The modern passion for breeding dogs has produced some exotic, even ridiculous crosses. Since the early 1990s, hybrid 'designer' breeds have proliferated, especially in the United States, much to the alarm of some who worry about the genetic implications. Among the many to have emerged in recent years are:

Bagel – Beagle and Basset Hound
Chug – Chihuahua and Pug
Cockapoo – Cocker Spaniel and Poodle
Doodleman Pinscher – Poodle and Doberman Pinscher
Eskipoo – Eskimo Dog and Poodle
Jug – Jack Russell Terrier and Pug
Labradoodle – Labrador and Poodle

Maltipoo – Maltese and Poodle
Puggle – Pug and Beagle
Pugshire – Pug and Yorkshire Terrier
Sharp Asset – Basset Hound and Shar-Pei

You Are What You Wear

How Cats and Dogs Are Colour-Coded

Many personality characteristics and physical attributes in cats and dogs are linked to genetic defects that also produce particular coat and skin colours.

Scientists, for instance, think the genetic defect that produces congenital deafness in both cats and dogs is linked to the one that produces all-white, spotted, roan and piebald coats.

As a result of this, white, roan and piebald dogs are more likely to be deaf than dogs with other coloured coats. For instance, 22 per cent of Dalmatians are deaf in one ear, while 8 per cent are deaf in both ears. Around 20 per cent of white Bull Terriers are deaf. The whiteness gene is also linked to blue eyes, so dogs with white coats and blue eyes are even more likely to be deaf. Almost half blue-eyed Dalmatians are deaf.

TORTOISESHELL CATS inherit the ginger patches from one parent and the dark patches from the other.

CATS WITH orange in their coat tend to be more aggressive.

MALE CATS with coloured coats are rare in communities of felines in urban environments. One theory has it that because they tend to be more aggressive they are also less successful at mating. Males who succeed in mating tend to be the ones who wait patiently for their turn. Cats with orange in their coat, in particular, lose out on chances to mate because they are too busy fighting.

NOT ALL white cats with blue eyes are deaf, but they are more likely to be deaf than other cats. White cats with one blue eye are usually deaf on the blue-eyed side.

BLACK CATS shouldn't be seen as symbols of bad luck – quite the opposite, in fact. Scientists have discovered that, if anything, black cats have a fortunate genetic make-up. The gene for melanism, which makes their fur black, may also be able to prevent certain viruses or bacteria from entering their cells, making them more resistant to disease than cats with lighter-coloured coats. Dark coats also act as a better camouflage for hunting.

Curiously, in humans, when a version of the same gene is mutated, it gives some people ginger hair.

ACCORDING TO one study, black cats are more tolerant of overcrowded human society.

RED SPELLS danger, at least when it comes to dogs' coats. In a major study of English Cocker Spaniels, the celebrated animal behaviourist Dr Roger Mugford revealed that 74 per cent – almost three out of four – of dogs referred to his clinic with behavioural problems were red- or golden-coloured dogs. When scientists at Cambridge and the University of Pennsylvania tested this further by looking at a group of more than 1,100 spaniels, they found the same thing.

Dogs with solid-coloured coats were more aggressive than those with mixed-coloured or partly coloured coats. Of those with solid coats, the red and golden spaniels were more aggressive than the black-coated ones.

A STUDY of eighty-four British Shorthair kittens found that those with red, cream and tortoiseshell coats made more escape attempts when handled by unfamiliar people.

PART NINE

It's a Cat and Dog's Life

Some Curious Truths About Canine and Feline Lifestyles

FOR CATS AND DOGS, daily life is largely a matter of mundane routine. There is, of course, a lot of eating and sleeping to do, but there is also lots of washing, grooming and toileting to attend to. No wonder, then, that they so look forward to their playtimes. Cats and dogs love nothing more than chasing a ball, watching a little television or listening to music. Some even feel the artistic urge themselves and start painting and composing music. After all this, of course, it's always important to get a good night's sleep. Even if – like most cats – you've already spent most of the day flat on your back.

All That Litters

Personal Hygiene in Cats and Dogs

Male and female dogs have very different toiletary habits. In general, females squat to urinate, while males cock their rear legs up and tilt their bodies to the side. They start doing this from around eight weeks old. Adult dogs have twelve different postures for urinating. Males have four variations, while females have eight even though they urinate less.

The cat's fastidious nature shows itself in its toiletary habits. Outdoors, most cats dig a small hole with their forepaws, then cover it up again when they have relieved themselves. Indoors, they will cover up in their litter tray in a similar fashion.

Cats will go to great lengths to keep themselves clean during all this. Kuiat cats have been observed standing on the four corners of a litter box so as to avoid contact. Cats can also easily learn to relieve themselves in their owner's toilet.

Some researchers believe that cats that bury their faeces are insecure. Cats communicate a lot of information through their body odour and the smell of faeces is a signal of aggression. Many cats bury their droppings underground so as to dampen the odour – and the signal it is sending out. Some cats, however, do the opposite. Studies of communities of feral cats revealed that dominant cats actually advertised their droppings, placing them on raised surfaces where the smell could circulate more easily. It was only weaker and less confident, lower-ranking cats that buried their faeces.

Cats soil their owner's home for a variety of reasons. Emotional upsets and stress, along with medical conditions like cystitis, can be a cause. Some vets, however, are convinced cats do make a mess on their owner's sofa, bedclothes or carpet out of pure vindictiveness. Cats often do this after being told off or when a new cat is introduced to the home, they think. They admit, though, that proving this will be extremely hard.

A MALE cat's wee is smellier than that of a female. The pungent smell of cat's urine is created by amino acids, one of which is known as felinine. A study found that males produce up to five times as much of this as females do each day.

THE AVERAGE dog deposits ¾ pound (0.35 kilograms) of faeces every day. On average a dog defecates between two and three times a day.

IN BRITAIN alone, dogs deposit 4.5 million litres of urine and 1 million kilograms of faeces every day.

DOGS ARE highly regular in their toilet habits. In general they will defecate twenty minutes after eating.

A STUDY of Beagles discovered that 23 per cent of defecations by males were directed towards a fence.

CATS EXPEND almost as much bodily fluid grooming themselves each day as they do urinating.

It's not surprising that cat owners get covered in cat hair. Cats can have up to two hundred hairs per square millimetre of skin. They also have three different types of hair.

Castrated male cats grow their hair long. A study revealed cats that remained intact groomed themselves more and kept their coats shorter than those who had been neutered. Scientists think the habit is linked to lower hormone levels.

Dogs have two types of hair, 'guard hair', which is coarse and protective, and 'down' hair, which provides insulation. Some breeds have been developed to have more of one type of hair. Yorkshire Terriers have less downy hair: one hundred hairs per square centimetre, compared with five hundred hairs per square centimetre in Nordic breeds of dog. Boxers have no downy hair and short guard hair.

Dogs go bald. Some breeds suffer pattern baldness and alopecia. As with humans, there is no known cure for baldness.

Dogs can get dandruff. They suffer from a condition

called seborrhoea in which the sebaceous glands that normally keep the coat well oiled instead produce flaky deposits much like human dandruff.

CATS ATTRACT more fleas than dogs do. A major study by UK vets in 2005 looked at the cases of more than 4,000 cats and dogs treated in thirty-one different practices. Flea infestations were present in more than 21 per cent of cats but less than 7 per cent of dogs.

DOGS ALSO suffer from DO, or Doggy Odour. Another form of seborrhoea produces too much oil in the dog's coat and makes the dog's coat greasy, sticky and extremely smelly.

CATS LOSE their hair when they are stressed. Nervous cats suffer from alopecia. Others lose their hair by constantly scratching the area around their ears with their hind feet.

CATS CAN also get eczema from excessive licking.

HAIRBALLS MAKE cats depressed. They also make them skinny. Because they groom so much, cats accumulate large amounts of hair on their tongue. When they swallow this it forms hairballs inside their digestive system. Usually cats get rid of them by vomiting or excretion, but sometimes hairballs remain inside their system. Vets have discovered this has several side-effects, including anorexia and depression.

Bite Me

How Cats and Dogs Play

YOUNG DOMESTIC dogs are much more playful than wild dogs. Beagle puppies in one study demonstrated play behaviour seven times more often than coyotes and three times as often as wolf cubs.

IN LITTERS, when one puppy invites another one to play the response is positive 77 per cent of the time.

LOTS OF puppies play at mounting one another. They climb on top of each other, roughly clasp on and thrust, as if practising sexual activities. More than 80 per cent of this type of behaviour is done by males. Females do climb on top of one another and behave roughly just as often as males, however.

Scientists have identified a signal in dogs that means 'let's play at fighting'. The signal involves one dog bowing to another by dropping on to its front paws and lowering its head. The dog that has signalled will then start fighting with the other one. Studies indicate this is a dog's way of telling its playmate it is about to attack but that this should not be misread as an aggressive act. In effect the dog is saying: 'Don't take this seriously, I'm fooling around.' Dogs sometimes repeat the signal midway through a fight, particularly if it gets very physical.

Puppies rarely play on their own if housed individually.

Puppies have a repertoire of play activities. The bulk of these, however, include biting and pawing one another. One study discovered that puppies bit each other in 87 per cent of their games.

Cats start playing at two weeks of age. They begin by attempting to bat moving objects.

At between four and sixteen weeks of age cats take part

in complex social play with their siblings. They play eight distinct games.

- **Belly up**, in which a kitten lies on its back making a pawing motion, with its mouth open and teeth bared.
- **Stand up**, in which one kitten stands over another kitten that is lying in a Belly-up position. The kittens may bite each other.
- **Side step**, in which one kitten turns side on to another kitten, arching its body and curving its tail up before walking towards the other kitten or circling it.
- **The pounce**, in which one kitten crouches low, then makes a sudden thrust forward towards another kitten.
- **Vertical stance**, in which the kitten tries to stand up and raise its front paws into the air.
- **Chase**, in which kittens pursue and run away from one another.
- **Horizontal leap**, in which the kitten suddenly leaps off the ground from a crouched position.
- **Face off**, in which two kittens sit staring intensely at each other and making pawing movements at each other's face. Kittens are so fond of this game they will often play it on their own.

Kittens also play individual games that prepare them for hunting prey as adults. Vets have identified several games, in which they practise particular attacking techniques. These are known as mouse, rabbit and bird. There is also a form of play in which a kitten will suddenly leap at an imaginary object and chase it around the ground or up a wall. This is known as hallucinatory play.

Adult cats hunt for fun. They will often play a cruel game in which they trap and release their prey. Cats have been observed playing 'baseball' with mice by batting and catching them. They have also been seen playing 'badminton' with birds by swatting them into the air like shuttlecocks.

Dogs need mental stimulation and get bored with toys. In a study of thirty-two rescue dogs given a series of squeaky balls, chews and tug ropes over a period of six days, the dogs spent only 8 per cent of the time playing with their toys. Their interest waned below this by the end of the six days.

Cats play more with toys when they are hungry. In a major study, cats were offered toys immediately after eating and again sixteen hours after food. They were much more interested in playing with the toys when they were hungry than immediately after eating. Scientists think this suggests cats are motivated by toys because they see them as potential prey.

When dogs play with humans, they like to share their toys. With other dogs, though, they're much more possessive and tend to keep toys to themselves, a study revealed.

Dogs are good winners but bad losers. When dogs beat their owners at something, they don't crow over it. Researchers at Southampton University found that when they staged tug-of-war matches with fourteen retrievers, and then pretended to lose, the dogs didn't show dominance behaviour such as trying to stand over their vanquished opponent. The dogs weren't great losers, though: if the scientist won the match, the dog was less likely to want to play again.

THE JOY OF REX

Some Things That Make Cats and Dogs Happy (and Sad)

CATS DEVELOP stress-related illnesses. A study at Edinburgh University discovered that a condition called feline idiopathic cystitis was exacerbated by stress. When they studied a sample of cats they saw that specific events triggered the cats' anxiety. Moving house and a newcomer joining their human family were major factors. But by far the most anxiety was caused when cats didn't get along with other felines in their home.

CATS HATE unpredictability. A study found that when they altered the routine of a group of eight cats, and left another group as they were, the cats who didn't know what was going on became chronically stressed. They became more alert, slept poorly and attempted to hide a lot.

Cats also get stressed by rejection. Another study conducted in shelters found that cats who had been abandoned by their owners tended to hide away at the back of their kennel, looking stressed, with their heads down and eyes wide open. Stray cats brought in off the street, however, lay around, looking much more relaxed and resting comfortably on their sides.

Abandoned cats are, as a result, less likely to find a new home and more likely to be put down.

Dogs laugh. While at play, they let out what scientist Patricia Simonet has described as 'a breathy, pronounced, forced exhalation'. While dogs also bark, growl and whine during play, this is the only sound that is exclusive to playtime. Simonet has concluded that this is the canine equivalent of a chuckle.

Dogs like the sound of laughter. When they hear a dog laugh, dogs adopt a 'play face' expression. Laughter also makes them more relaxed. In an experiment a group of dogs in an animal shelter became significantly less

stressed and more sociable when they heard recordings of dog laughter played.

DOGS RESPOND to the sound of human whispers. In studies, well over half of the dogs that were invited to play with a gentle whisper responded immediately. Scientists think this is because they associate the whisper with the canine laugh, which produces a similar exhalation of air.

CATS DON'T laugh. The strange curling of the top lip they perform may look like an expression of amusement but in fact this is a method of heightening their sense of smell during the mating season. The technique, known as the Flehmen Response, is common in horses, zebras and donkeys too.

When cats want to find out information about other cats, they raise their upper lips and hold their mouths slightly open. By doing so they carry the scent directly into the vomeronasal organ, where they process information, in particular about a potential mate's fitness and fertility.

Cats do signal happiness in different ways, however. They perform a kneading action with their paws. The action is known by various names, from skronking and paddy pawing to making muffins.

As with some humans, having the television on in the background makes dogs feel happier and calmer.

In one major study, scientists observed the way fifty rescue-centre dogs responded to having a television screen on in their living quarters. The television showed different images: sometimes a blank screen; at other times, images of dogs, other animals and humans. The dogs spent only around 10 per cent of the time watching television, but when they did pay attention they spent more time looking at moving images than at a blank screen, although they got bored with each of the sets of images as time went by.

Having the television on, however, did significantly reduce the amount of noise the dogs made. Because of their heightened ability to see moving lines, dogs don't see television in the same way as humans. But scientists think even the visual stimulation provided by a flickering image is enough to calm dogs down.

ONE SCIENTIST cites the case of a dog-care centre that has found three particular types of programmes that keep their inmates in a good mood. They are comedies starring the Three Stooges and the Marx Brothers, and Westerns.

WHEREAS DOGS like Westerns, cats prefer the Discovery Channel. Studies have found that cats are drawn to moving images of other animals. One experiment showed cats two computers, one containing fourteen moving dots that represented the outline of a running or walking cat and a similar number of dots moving randomly around the screen. The cats paid much more attention to the screen containing cats.

Intriguingly, when the images were shown upside down the cats weren't interested in either. Scientists think this is because cats can't conceive of any logical reason why animals would be upside down.

This would explain why many owners report their cats being drawn to nature programmes on television. Scientists think they are able to make out the images of animals and are attracted by the potential prey they represent.

DOGS PREFER Bach to Britney. A study by Queen's University in Belfast looked at the way hundreds of distressed rescue dogs reacted to different kinds of music. The sound of human voices and pop music by artists like Britney Spears did nothing to calm the stressed dogs down. Heavy metal and grunge music made the dogs even more agitated. When the band Metallica was played, for instance, the dogs started barking loudly.

At the other end of the scale, however, the scientists discovered that dogs relaxed and enjoyed themselves most when they were played classical music. Naturally, they liked the sound of Bach in particular.

BACH, YES; barking, no. The excessive noise in animal shelters, where the sound of dogs can be louder than that of a road drill, can 'physically stress dogs and lead to behavioural, physiological and anatomical responses', one study concluded.

Play It Again, Tom

When Cats Play Piano, Dogs Howl Along

Cats make musical instruments. When the King of Spain visited Brussels in 1549 he was entertained by a bear playing an organ. Instead of pipes the organ had twenty small boxes, each containing a cat whose tail was sticking out. By pressing one of these keys the bear produced an 'infernal gallemaufry o' din'. Cat organs were still in use in Prague in 1773. One particularly nasty version had keys which, when pressed, drove pointed barbs into the base of the cats' tails.

Cats and dogs featured in musical compositions. In 1608 the Italian Adriano Banchieri wrote a *contrapunto bestiale al mente* (an improvised counterpoint with beasts). It featured a cat and a dog – along with a cuckoo and an owl.

CATS CAN compose music. The composer Scarlatti was inspired when his cat walked across the keyboard of his piano. He hurriedly copied down the notes and called the piece 'The Cat's Fugue'. The piece was hailed as a masterpiece by another great composer, Liszt.

CATS CAN 'play' piano. Domestic cats have been known to play the keyboard with both paws, often producing passable melodies and chord structures. A film of a cat called Nora playing with both paws sparked a fierce debate after millions watched her playing along with her owner on the internet.

YOU COULD call it perfect bitch. There is strong evidence to suggest that dogs can tell the difference between musical notes.

In the wild, for instance, packs of wolves join in a chorus of howling when they link up together. But studies of the individual voices have revealed that each wolf sings in a slightly different register. If a wolf hears another one howling the same note as it is singing, it will deliberately adjust its tone so that it is different.

Scientists think this is why domestic dogs sing slightly out of tune when they join in with human music. The dog is deliberately trying to be heard.

SOME FAMOUS musicians have been convinced that dogs have a musical ear. Edward Elgar, composer of the anthem 'Land of Hope and Glory', was friendly with a Bulldog called Dan, who belonged to the organist at Hereford Cathedral. Elgar told how, during choir practice, Dan used to growl at choristers that were out of tune.

CATS PAINT. Given a set of oils and an easel, cats happily create colourful designs. Some observers believe that this indicates a strong aesthetic streak and are convinced cats are often creating works that represent their view of their world around them.

So convinced of the cat's creative genius are some, that several books on cat 'art' have analysed the different schools of feline painting. These range from conventional categories like traditional portrait painting and abstract expressionism to more unusual genres such as romantic ruralism, psychometric impressionism, elemental fragmentism and spontaneous reductionism. Cats have also been hailed for their ability to create 'nocturnal installations'. One, by a cat named Radar, was a Damian Hirst-style work featuring two dead mice left together on a carpet.

DOGS CREATE their own masterpieces too. A Jack Russell called Tillie from Brooklyn has had solo exhibitions of her work held in Milan, Amsterdam, Brussels and Bermuda. In all, more than a hundred of her abstract expressionist works have sold, with one fetching $2,200. Tillie usually produces her paintings – or paw prints, as her owner, Bowman Hastie, calls them – in fifteen minutes.

Let Sleeping Dogs Snore

How Cats and Dogs Catch Forty Winks

CATS SLEEP for two thirds of their lives. This is twice as much as most other mammals.

Given the amount of time they devote to slumbering, it is hardly surprising that cats dream. Electroencephalographs, or EEGs, of sleeping cats have detected rapid eye movement, or REM, the standard sign of dreaming.

Cats tend to alternate between REM sleep and a lighter, or slow-wave, sleep. They spend six or seven minutes out of every half-hour in the 'dreaming state' before spending the next twenty to thirty minutes in slow-wave sleep. This means that cats spend 50 per cent of their lives in a lighter, or slow-wave, sleep. It also means they spend 15 per cent of their lives dreaming.

SOME DOGS are narcoleptic. Dobermans were bred by a German tax-collector who wanted to produce a dog so fierce that it could protect him on travels through bandit-infested countryside and persuade reluctant debtors to pay up.

One line of the breed didn't quite work out according to plan, however. This unfortunate strain of Dobermans suffer from narcolepsy – an inherited condition that makes them drop sound asleep whenever they get excited. Even the sight or smell of a favourite snack is enough to send them into a deep slumber.

DOGS ALSO dream. In tests, vets have observed them experiencing REM sleep.

Like cats, dogs tend to sleep in on–off patterns, snoozing for an hour, then being awake for half an hour. During this period they are often highly active, displaying behaviour from pacing around to barking at other dogs. Whether this is connected to the dreams or not no one knows.

SOME 21 per cent of dogs snore. Only 7 per cent of cats do so.

AFTERWORD

THERE ARE, IT SEEMS, no lengths to which enquiring minds will not go in order to understand our closest animal companions.

Take, for example, the work currently being carried out by a New York vet called Robert Lopez. Mr Lopez recently announced that, in order to investigate the effect of ear mites on cats, he has collected a sample of the microscopic insects from patients at his surgery and plans to insert them into his own ear. The scientific world is just itching to know what he discovers.

In the meantime, we will continue to be treated to other even more surprising insights. Studies into the way cats and dogs think, communicate, reproduce, navigate and predict events beyond our own meagre comprehension are being conducted in universities and research laboratories around the world. Who knows, one day we might even get to know what they think of us.

Of one thing we can be sure, however. For every answered question there will always be an unsolved riddle. It is, for instance, now widely accepted that dogs laugh. But that raises another question. What is it that tickles a dog's funny bone? And is it true, as Charles Darwin's friend George Romanes argued back in the nineteenth century, that nothing is more certain to produce a canine chuckle than a 'good joke'?

Now, there's one study we are all *really* itching to read.

Acknowledgements

MY FIRST thanks must go to the real scientists: the assorted behaviourists, vets, zoologists and ethologists who are expanding our knowledge of the animal world – and cats and dogs, in particular – on a daily basis. It is the fruits of their rigorous, painstaking labours that I have plundered so liberally to produce this book. I am grateful to them all.

Dr Steve Le Comber, an evolutionary biologist at the School of Biological and Chemical Sciences, Queen Mary, University of London, was, as often before, an ever-willing source of help, but this time his greatest contribution was to put me in touch with a colleague of his, Elli Leadbeater. Elli was an invaluable research assistant as I trawled around for material suitable for this book. Her gift for turning up obscure – and, often, ancient – texts was invaluable, as was her scepticism about some of the more eccentric studies that had caught my less-stringent eye. Elli, for instance, debunked a very funny but ultimately bogus study that claimed to have discovered that cats have an adverse reaction to men with beards. It was a close shave . . . I nearly fell for it.

I must say thanks again to my agent Mary Pachnos and all at Aitken Alexander. At Transworld I am fortunate indeed to be published by Francesca Liversidge. Thanks too to Nick Robinson and Zoe Hood for their enthusiasm for this book and, once again, to Stephanie von Reiswitz for her wonderful illustrations.

Finally, as ever, I owe my biggest thanks to my family, Cilene, Gabriella and Thomas, each of whom displays a faith in me that would put even the most devoted Labrador to shame. I'd be lost without them.

REFERENCES

Key to Abbreviations

AABS	*Applied Animal Behaviour Science*
AB	*Animal Behaviour*
AZ	*American Zoologist*
CP	*Canine Practice*
FP	*Feline Practice*
JAVMA	*Journal of the American Veterinary Medicine Association*
JCP	*Journal of Comparative Psychology*
JFMS	*Journal of Feline Medicine & Surgery*
NS	*New Scientist*

PART ONE

Sense and Scent Ability: How Cats and Dogs Smell, Hear, See and Feel

You Stink, Therefore I Am: How Cats and Dogs Smell (pages 5–10)

'Dogs can smell human fingerprints': *AB*, vol. 12, 1964, pp. 311–15.

'Can even smell electricity': *Quarterly Review of Biology*, vol. 3, (1), 1928, p. 28.

'Can tell from the smell of a cow's urine': T. D. Wyatt, *Pheromones and Animal Behaviour*, Cambridge University Press, 2002, p. 253.

'Smell is the first sense that a cat develops': *AB*, vol. 23, 1975, pp. 368–74; Beaver, *Veterinary Aspects of Feline Behaviour*, C. V. Mosby, St Louis, 1980, p. 20.

'The nose pad of a cat': J. Ronald Galli, Weber State University, Utah, reported by Ontario Association of Physics Teachers, www.oapt.ca.

'Dogs really can smell fear': *JAVMA*, vol. 155, 1969, pp. 1995-6.

'Dogs can detect odours that are up to 40 feet underground': S. Coren, *How Dogs Think: Understanding the Canine Mind*, Pocket Books, London, 2005, p. 96; US Department of Agriculture publications.

'The source of the dog's exceptional ability': S. Coren, *How Dogs Think: Understanding the Canine Mind*, Pocket Books, London, 2005, p. 67.

'Smell is the dog's dominant sense': S. Coren, *How Dogs Think: Understanding the Canine Mind*, Pocket Books, London, 2005, p. 63; *AABS*, reported in *The Sunday Times*, *News Review*, 6 Nov. 2005.

'The cat's olfactory bulb': *FP*, vol. 7, no. 8, Sep. 1977.

'A young kitten that becomes distressed': *Scientific American*, vol. 227, 1972, pp. 18–25.

'Both dogs and cats have an extrasensory organ': *Philosophical Transactions of the Royal Society B: Biological Sciences*, vol. 361, no. 1476, 29 Dec. 2006, pp. 2061–78.

'Dogs react in different ways to different smells': *AABS*, vol. 91, pp. 143–53.

'Cats also respond to different smells': *AABS*, vol. 85, pp. 107–19.

'As far as dogs are concerned, every human has a unique smell': T. D. Wyatt, *Pheromones and Animal Behaviour*, Cambridge University Press, 2002, p. 274.

'As a result of this, dogs can track human smells over long distances': T. D. Wyatt, *Pheromones and Animal Behaviour*, Cambridge University Press, 2002, p. 218.

'Scientists who tested four German Shepherds': T. D. Wyatt, *Pheromones and Animal Behaviour*, Cambridge University Press, 2002, p. 218.

'The reason why dogs have black noses': *NS*, vol. 188, no. 2529, 10 Dec. 2005.

The Cat's Whispers: How Felines and Canines Tune In to the World Around Them (pages 11–13)

'Cats have more than twenty muscles': D. C. Turner & P. Bateson (eds), *The Domestic Cat: The Biology of its Behaviour*, Cambridge University Press, 1988, p. 152; R. Tabor, *The Wild Life of the Domestic Cat*, Arrow Books, London, 1983.

'Cats can pinpoint the source of sounds with amazing accuracy': M. Pollard, *The Encyclopedia of Cats*, Paragon, 1999.

'Cats are capable of hearing a greater range of frequencies': C. Thorne (ed.): *The Waltham Book of Cat and Dog Behaviour*, Pergamon Press, Oxford, 1992, p. 40; M. & F. Sunquist, *Wild Cats of the World*, University of Chicago Press, 2002, p. 10.

'The adult cat's ability to distinguish other animals' sounds': *Saugetierkundliche Mitteilungen*, vol. 15, 1967, pp. 169–70.

'Many owners think their cats somehow sense their arrival home': M. Pollard, *The Encyclopedia of Cats*, Paragon, 1999.

'Using their swivelling ears': Beaver, *Canine Behaviour: A Guide for Veterinarians*, W. B. Saunders, Philadelphia, 1999, p. 50; Fay & Popper, *Comparative Hearing: Mammals*, Springer-Verlag, 1994.

'Dogs can hear both ultra- and subsonic sound': S. Coren, *How Dogs Think: Understanding the Canine Mind*, Pocket Books, London, 2005, pp. 144–5.

What's Blue, Pussycat?: How Cats and Dogs See (pages 14–19)

'Because of its history as a predator': *JAVMA*, vol. 207, no. 12, 15 Dec. 1995, pp. 1623–34.

'The elliptical pupil of a cat's eye': *Journal of Experimental Biology*, vol. 209, pp. 18–25.

'Cat's eyes shine when they get caught in the beam of a light': *JAVMA*, vol. 207, no. 12, pp. 1623–34.

'Cats can be used as rudimentary clocks': D. C. Turner & P. Bateson (eds), *The Domestic Cat: The Biology of its Behaviour*, Cambridge University Press, 1988, p. 184.

'Siamese cats are often born with double vision': M. Pollard, *The Encyclopedia of Cats*, Paragon, 1999.

'Cats have great peripheral vision': M. & F. Sunquist, *Wild Cats of the World*, University of Chicago Press, 2002, p. 10.

'The cat family is reckoned to have the best binocular vision': M. & F. Sunquist, *Wild Cats of the World*, University of Chicago Press, 2002, p. 9.

'Domestic cats are slightly near-sighted': C. Thorne (ed.), *The Waltham Book of Cat and Dog Behaviour*, Pergamon Press, Oxford, 1992, pp. 41–2.

'Feral cats, however, tend to be long-sighted': C. Thorne (ed.), *The Waltham Book of Cat and Dog Behaviour*, Pergamon Press, Oxford, 1992, pp. 41–2.

'Cats have a blind spot, right under their nose': Beaver, *Veterinary Aspects of Feline Behaviour*, C. V. Mosby, St Louis, 1980, p. 13.

'Dogs aren't colour-blind': *Visual Neuroscience*, vol. 3, pp. 119–25.

'When presented with different shades of grey': *Journal of Vision*, vol. 4, pp. 241–9.

'Cats can see limited amounts of colour': M. & F. Sunquist, *Wild Cats of the World*, University of Chicago Press, 2002, p. 9.

'Dogs can detect flickering lights at a high frequency': *JAVMA*, vol. 207, no. 12, pp. 1623–34, 15 Dec. 1995.

'Both cats and dogs are equipped with windscreen wipers': Bruce Fogle, *Caring for Your Dog*, Dorling Kindersley, London, 2002, p. 214; University of Michigan Museum of Zoology, Animal Diversity Web, http://animaldiversity.ummz.umich.edu.

'Dogs have, on average, 20 : 75 vision': *JAVMA*, vol. 207, no. 12, pp. 1623–34, 15, Dec. 1995

'Dogs have a large blind spot behind their heads': Beaver, *Canine Behaviour: A Guide for Veterinarians*, W. B. Saunders, Philadelphia, 1999, p. 45.

'Dogs also don't have great "depth of field" to their vision': S. Coren, *How Dogs Think: Understanding the Canine Mind*, Pocket Books, London, 2005, p. 24.

'. . . can see things at great distances': *JAVMA*, vol. 207, no. 12, pp. 1623–34, 15 Dec. 1995.

I Feel Kitty: How Cats and Dogs Touch and Feel (pages 20–4)

'Cats' and dogs' sense of touch is concentrated around their snouts': C. Thorne (ed.), *The Waltham Book of Cat and Dog Behaviour*, Pergamon Press, Oxford, 1992, pp. 35–6; R. F. Ewer, *The Carnivores*, Weidenfeld & Nicolson, London, 1973; S. Coren, *How Dogs Think: Understanding the Canine Mind*, Pocket Books, London, 2005, p. 122.

'Cats also have vibrissae on their front paws': *Acta Physiol. Scand.* vol. 77, pp. 396–416, and vol. 65, pp. 364–9; *Proceedings of the Zoological Society of London*, vol. 1, pp. 127–36.

'Cats use their vibrissae to determine if a space is too small to squeeze through': C. Thorne (ed.), *The Waltham Book of Cat and Dog Behaviour*, Pergamon Press, Oxford, 1992, p. 35.

'Male dogs tend to be left-pawed': *Behavioural Brain Research*, vol. 153, no. 2, pp. 521–5, 31 Aug. 2004. *Behavioural Processes*, vol. 61, no. 1–2, pp. 27–35, 28 Feb. 2003.

'Cats, on the other hand, are generally left-pawed': *Journal of Comparative Physiology and Psychology*, vol. 48, pp. 137–40.

'The pads of a dog's feet are equipped': S. Coren, *How Dogs Think: Understanding the Canine Mind*, Pocket Books, London, 2005, pp. 119–20.

'Puppies have special, heat-seeking sensors': S. Coren, *How Dogs Think: Understanding the Canine Mind*, Pocket Books, London, 2005, p. 118; Y. Zotterman, *Sensory Mechanisms*, Elsevier, New York, 1967.

'Why was the cat on a hot tin roof?': M. Pollard, *The*

Encyclopedia of Cats, Paragon, 1999.

'How hot is that doggie in the window?': *Journal of Mammology*, vol. 58, pp. 74–8.

'Their limited ability to cool themselves down': S. Coren, *How Dogs Think: Understanding the Canine Mind*, Pocket Books, London, 2005, p. 66.

'Cats lick themselves to protect against': Desmond Morris, *Catwatching*, Ebury Press, 2002, p. 25.

Is It Raining, Cats and Dogs?: Canine and Feline Superpowers (pages 25–35)

'Dogs can detect cancer': *AABS*, vol. 89, (1-2), pp. 107–16; *The Sunday Times*, *News Review*, 6 Nov. 2005.

'They can also learn to anticipate when a person is going to have an epileptic fit': *Seizure*, vol. 8, pp. 62–5; *National Geographic*, 11 Feb. 2004.

'Cats may also have the ability to sense epileptic fits': *BBC News*, 13 June 2006; http://news.bbc.co.uk/1/hi/england/south_yorkshire/5076338.stml.

'It remains a mystery': *National Geographic*, 11 Feb. 2004; *Neurology*, 23 Jan. 2007.

'Cats have, historically, been regarded as valuable weather forecasters': Angela Sayer & Howard Loxton, *Encyclopedia of the Cat*, Hamlyn, London, 1999, pp. 23–4.

'Their ultra-sensitive vibrissae': Angela Sayer & Howard Loxton, *Encyclopedia of the Cat*, Hamlyn, London, 1999, pp. 23–4.

'Dogs too are particularly sensitive to changes in the weather': *CP*, vol. 4, no. 4, p. 6.

'As with cats, dogs also get nervous about noises': Beaver, *Canine Behaviour: A Guide for Veterinarians*, W. B. Saunders, Philadelphia, 1999, p. 85.

'Cats and dogs may be able to sense earthquakes': *NS*, vol. 193, no. 2591, 17 Feb. 2007.

'In the USA a study found that': *Science*, vol. 208, no. 4445, 16 May 1980, pp. 695–6.

'Before the Asian tsunami struck on 26 December 2004': *National Geographic* online, 4 Jan. 2005.

'Some cats' hair stands on end in the run-up to earthquakes': *Feline Practice*, vol. 7, no. 8, p. 10, 12 Nov. 1977; *Vet. Med. Small Animal Clin.*, vol. 73, pp. 834 and 836, June 1978.

'Big-headed dogs don't hear earthquakes coming': *NS*, vol. 193, no. 2591, 17 Feb. 2007.

'Dogs are able to sense gunfire': *Praxis Veterinaria*, vol. 51, no. 3, 2003.

'Cats and dogs may possess telepathic powers': Sheldrake, *Dogs That Know When Their Owners Are Coming Home*, Hutchinson, London, 1999, p. xiii.

'Sheldrake believes . . . morphic fields': Sheldrake, *Dogs That Know When Their Owners Are Coming Home*, Hutchinson, London, 1999, p. 257.

'Dogs are better than cats': Sheldrake, *Dogs That Know When Their Owners Are Coming Home*, Hutchinson, London, 1999, p. 52.

'The mainstream scientific community are sceptical': S. Coren,

How Dogs Think, pp. 152–7.

'Cats seem to hypnotize other creatures': M. & F. Sunquist, *Wild Cats of the World*, University of Chicago Press, 2002, p. 105; *Science*, vol. xix, no. 471, 12 Feb. 1982, pp. 95–6.

'Dogs, on the other hand, seem to be susceptible to hypnosis by other animals': *Science*, vol. xix, no. 471, 12 Feb. 1982, pp. 95–6.

PART TWO

What's the Dog for Cat?: The Curious Truth About Canine and Feline Communication

Snap, Gurgle and Puff: Pet Sounds and What They Really Mean (pages 41–8)

'A dog's bark': *American Journal of Veterinary Research*, vol. 24, no. 100, 1963, p. 415.

'A Beagle was once recorded': *Smithsonian*, vol. 21, no. 10, p. 119.

'Hungry cats have been known': *Experimental Brain Research*, vol. 89, pp. 333–40.

'Purring is one of the very few natural sounds': *Respiration Physiology*, vol. 16, pp. 351–61.

'Cats can purr continuously for up to two hours': J. L. Gittleman (ed.), *Carnivore Behaviour, Ecology and Evolution*, Chapman & Hall; *Acta Zoologica Fennica*, vol. 171, pp. 83–8.

'According to a study, only two out of three dogs': *AABS*, vol. 36, p. 233.

'Sleeping dogs are more alert': *AABS*, vol. 39, p. 151.

'Dogs living in groups are more likely to bark than dogs living on their own': *AABS*, vol. 39, p. 151.

'A dog's bark can be just as bad as its bite': *Kawabata*, vol. I, 2000; *Jibi Inkoka Tokeibu Geka*, vol. 72, pp. 115–18.

'The Basenji': www.basenji.com.

'A distant relative, the yodelling dingo': *NS*, vol. 131, no. 1784, 31 Aug. 1991.

'Dogs can tell a lot from the tone of each other's growls': *Journal of Experimental Biology*, no. 202, pp. 2859–67.

'Among feral dogs, different sounds produce different responses': Bekoff & Allen, 1998.

'Some dogs have a word for cat': *NS*, vol. 183, no. 2455, 10 July 2004.

'Adult cats can make up to a dozen different types of call': D. C. Turner & P. Bateson (eds), *The Domestic Cat: The Biology of its Behaviour*, Cambridge University Press, 1988, p. 71.

'Cats have a secret, high-frequency alarm signal': *Biologische Zentrallblatt*, vol. 94, pp. 187–204; J. L. Gittleman (ed.), *Carnivore Behaviour, Ecology and Evolution*, Chapman & Hall.

'In the wild, only puppies bark': *NS*, vol. 182, no. 2451, 12 June 2004.

'Wild cats usually don't meow': Brown, *The Social Behaviour of Neutered Domestic Cats (Felis catus)*, University of Southampton Ph.D. thesis, 1993.

'Puppies can't bark': *AZ*, vol. 10, 1970, p. 293.

'Dogs puff': *American Journal of Veterinary Research*, vol. 24, no. 100, p. 415, 1963.

'Dogs make a snapping sound': M. W. Fox, *Understanding Your Cat*, Coward, McCann & Geoghegan, New York, 1974.

'Male dogs have a special whine': *American Journal of Veterinary Research*, vol. 24, no. 100, p. 415.

'Cats make a range of sounds': D. C. Turner & P. Bateson (eds), *The Domestic Cat: The Biology of its Behaviour*, Cambridge University Press, 1988, pp. 81–6.

'A cat's murmur': *Praxis Veterinaria*, vol. 51. no. 3, 2003.

'Cats have worked out': *JCP*, vol. 117, pp. 44–52.

'In 2001, Japanese researchers': *BBC News*, 8 August 2001.

Have I Got Poohs for You: How Actions Speak Louder Than Words (pages 49–55)

'Dogs talk through their backsides': Bruce Fogle, *Caring for Your Dog*, Dorling Kindersley, London, 2002, p. 290.

'Dogs cock their legs to urinate': J. L. Gittleman (ed.), *Carnivore Behaviour, Ecology and Evolution*, Chapman & Hall; *Journal of Mammology*, vol. 53, pp. 791–806.

'Tomcats spray all around their territory': D. C. Turner & P. Bateson (eds), *The Domestic Cat: The Biology of its Behaviour*, Cambridge University Press, 1988; M. & F. Sunquist, *Wild Cats of the World*, University of Chicago Press, 2002, p. 12.

'All adult tomcats produce their own distinctive scent': D. C. Turner & P. Bateson (eds), *The Domestic Cat: The Biology of its Behaviour*, Cambridge University Press, 1988.

'When cats rub themselves against objects': *Zeitschrift Tierphysiologie*, vol. 42, pp. 86–109; D. C. Turner & P. Bateson (eds), *The Domestic Cat: The Biology of its Behaviour*, Cambridge University Press, 1988.

'Cats also send messages via a scratch-and-sniff code': *AABS*, vol. 93, pp. 97–109.

'Cats may physically write each other messages too': D. C. Turner & P. Bateson (eds), *The Domestic Cat: The Biology of its Behaviour*, Cambridge University Press, 1988, p. 79.

'Happy dogs wag to the right': *Current Biology*, 20 March 2007, reported in *New York Times*, 25 April 2007.

'Cats signal friendship by sticking their tails up in the air': University of Southampton Ph.D. thesis, 1997, cited in D. C. Turner & P. Bateson (eds), *The Domestic Cat: The Biology of its Behaviour*, Cambridge University Press, 1988, pp. 87–8.

'Cats can signal that they want to play': *JFMS*, vol. 6, pp. 19–28.

'A cat's aggressive body language': D. C. Turner & P. Bateson (eds), *The Domestic Cat: The Biology of its Behaviour*, Cambridge University Press, 1988, pp. 72–3.

'Both dogs and cats conduct staring matches': J. A. Serpell (ed.), *The Domestic Dog: Its Evolution, Behaviour and Interactions with People*, Cambridge University Press, 1995; *JFMS*, vol. 6, pp. 19–28.

'Cats blink to signal': D. C. Turner & P. Bateson (eds), *The Domestic Cat: The Biology of its Behaviour*, Cambridge University Press, 1988; p. 233.

'Dogs puff themselves up': Beaver, *Canine Behaviour: A Guide*

for Veterinarians, W. B. Saunders, Philadelphia, 1999, p. 116.
'Dogs show dominance': Beaver, *Canine Behaviour: A Guide for Veterinarians*, W. B. Saunders, Philadelphia, 1999, p. 119.
'Dogs win confrontations': J. A. Serpell (ed.), *The Domestic Dog: Its Evolution, Behaviour and Interactions with People*, Cambridge University Press, 1995.

PART THREE

Who's a Clever Boy, Then? Some Truths About Canine and Feline Intelligence

Dogs Remember, Cats Don't Forget: Mental Agility (pages 61–6)

'Dogs have better short-term memories than cats': *Animal Cognition*, vol. 9, pp. 62–70; *Animal Cognition*, vol. 6, pp. 1–10.
'Intriguingly, however, cats performed much better': N. Maier & T. Schneirla, *Principles of Animal Psychology*, Dover Publications, 1965; www.catsinternational.org.
'Dogs remember their master's voice': *Animal Cognition*, vol. 10, pp. 17–21.
'John Lubbock' and 'Van': *Nature*, vol. 2, pp. 547–8.
'Fellow': *The Quarterly Review of Biology*, vol. 3, pp. 1–28.
'Cats can also perform similar feats of memory': www.messybeast.com/intelligence.htm.
'The most remarkable dog of the early twenty-first century': *Science*, vol. 304, pp. 1682–3.

'Female dogs have a lower boredom threshold': *Perception*, vol. 29, pp. 111–15.

One, Two, Three o'Clock, Four o'Clock – Snack: How Cats and Dogs Count, Tell the Time and Do Calculus (pages 67–77)

'Cats are exceptional timekeepers': *Acta Neurobiologiae Experimentalis*, vol. 36, 1976, pp. 311–17.

'Cats are also experts at time management': *Acta Neurobiologiae Experimentalis*, vol. 36, 1976, pp. 311–17.

'Dogs can tell the time too': I. Pavlov, *Essential Works of Pavlov*, Bantam Books, New York, 1966.

'Another Russian scientist': V. S. Rusinov, *Electrophysiology of the Central Nervous System*, Plenum Press, New York, 1970.

'Dogs can count – up to three, at least': *Animal Cognition*, vol. 5, pp. 183–6.

'Dogs know when they're outnumbered': J. A. Serpell (ed.) *The Domestic Dog: Its Evolution, Behaviour, and Interactions with People*, Cambridge University Press, pp. 199–216.

'Dogs do calculus': *May 2003 College Mathematics Journal & Science News*, vol. 163, no. 23, 7 June 2003.

'Perhaps curiosity did kill the cat': Bruce Fogle, *The Cat's Mind*, Pelham Books, London, 1991, p. 15.

'The ten brightest breeds of dog': S. Coren, *How Dogs Think: Understanding the Canine Mind*, Pocket Books, London, 2005, pp. 249–50.

'Cat intelligence rankings': Animal Planet www.animalplanet.com.

Not-so-dumb Mutts: Some Other Curious Feats of Canine and Feline Intelligence (pages 78–81)

'Dogs know how to medicate themselves': *Vet. Med. Small Animal Clin.* vol. 76, no. 7, p. 968.

'Dog saliva is an effective medicine': *Physiological Behaviour*, vol. 48, no. 3, p. 383.

'The cat's purr may be a self-healing mechanism': *National Geographic*, Jan. 2001, p. 11; *Chinese Journal of Surgery*, vol. 32, no. 4, 1994, pp. 217–19; *New Zealand Veterinary Journal*, 1973; *JAVMA*, vol. 214, no. 9, pp. 1336–41.

'Cats impersonate snakes': Desmond Morris, *Catwatching*, Ebury Press, 2002, p. 45.

'A cat in the USA, for instance, dialled 911': *Daily Telegraph*, online news, 5 Jan. 2006.

'Cats can raise the alarm in other ways too': *BBC News* online, 29 Dec. 2006.

PART FOUR

Is She Really Going Out with Them? The Truth About Cat and Dog Relationships

While the Tomcat's Away, the Wife's at Play: Cats, Dogs and the Mating Game (pages 87–92)

'Cats are highly promiscuous': *Behavioural Processes*, vol. 43, pp. 239–49.

'Female cats can be nymphomaniacs': Beaver, *Veterinary Aspects of Feline Behaviour*, C. V. Mosby, St Louis, 1980, p. 133.

'Tomcats remain lotharios even in old age': *Veterinary Record*, vol. 71, 26 Dec. 1959, pp. 966–78.

'The feline world's equivalent of Casanova is an Italian': *Behavioural Processes*, vol. 37, 1966, pp. 85–8.

'Some female cats are easier than others': *Aggressive Behaviour*, vol. 26, no. 6, 2000, pp. 455–65.

'Male cats appear to be possessive and certainly don't like the idea of sharing': *Proceedings of the Royal Society of London, Series B, Biological Sciences*, vol. 268, no. 1471, 22 May 2001, pp. 1049–53.

'Females like older, fatter cats': D. C. Turner & P. Bateson (eds), *The Domestic Cat: The Biology of its Behaviour*, Cambridge University Press, 1988, p. 139.

'Female cats can reach puberty': *Journal of Small Animal Practice*, vol. 18, pp. 31–7.

'Male dogs are obsessed with bottoms': *Anthrozoos*, vol. 5, pp. 245–53.

'Unlike most cats, dogs are extremely choosy': *AB*, vol. 15, pp. 546–58.

'In communities of wild dogs': *AABS*, vol. 13, (1–2), p. 113.

'When push comes to shove': S. McHugh, *Dog*, Reaktion Books, 2004.

'Male sexual activity drops in autumn': Beaver, *Veterinary Aspects of Feline Behaviour*, C. V. Mosby, St Louis, 1980, p. 114.

'Homosexuality is common in dogs': Bruce Bagemihl, *Biological Exuberance, Animal Homosexuality & Natural Diversity*, Profile Books, London, 1999, p. 81.

'This behaviour may have been inherited': Bruce Bagemihl, *Biological Exuberance, Animal Homosexuality & Natural Diversity*, Profile Books, London, 1999, p. 81.

'Dogs can be bisexual': B. P. O'Donoghue, *My Lead Dog Was a Lesbian*, Vintage, New York, 1996, p. 42.

'Cats have gay and lesbian affairs too': Bruce Bagemihl, *Biological Exuberance, Animal Homosexuality & Natural Diversity*, Profile Books, London, 1999, p. 81.

'This too may be rooted in their ancestry': Bruce Bagemihl, *Biological Exuberance, Animal Homosexuality & Natural Diversity*, Profile Books, London, 1999, p. 434.

Heavy Petting: Some Truths About Cat and Dog Sex (pages 93–7)

'Cat sex lasts for between one and four minutes': *Behaviour*, vol. 20, pp. 321–42.

'One major study of the sexual activity of male cats': *Journal of Comparative Physiological Psychology*, vol. 49, 1956, p. 321.

'A pair of cats': Beaver, *Veterinary Aspects of Feline Behaviour*, C. V. Mosby, St Louis, 1980, p. 117.

'Despite their insatiable appetite': *JFMS*, vol. 6, pp. 19–28.

'Dog sex can, by contrast, go on for hours': Beaver, *Canine Behaviour: A Guide for Veterinarians*, W. B. Saunders, Philadelphia, 1999, p. 205; J. Fennell, *The Seven Ages of Man's Best Friend*, HarperCollins, London, 2005.

'When the tie is finally broken': J. Fennell, *The Seven Ages of Man's Best Friend*, HarperCollins, London, 2005.

'Canine sex is a tricky business': *AABS*, vol. 13, (1–2), p. 113.
'Sex is a noisy business in the feline world': *Journal of Small Animal Practice*, vol. 18, Jan. 1977, pp. 31–7.
'The screeching, ear-splitting noise': Beaver, *Veterinary Aspects of Feline Behaviour*, C. V. Mosby, St Louis, 1980, p. 117.
'Dogs experience orgasms': E. P. Boas & E. F. Goldschmidt, *The Heart Rate*, C. C. Thomas, 1932; http://www.verrueckte-experimente.de/leseproben_e.html.
'Male dogs can suffer psychological trauma': *NS*, vol. 152, no. 2054, 2 Nov. 1996.
'Male tortoiseshell and calico cats': M. Fox, *Abnormal Behavior in Animals*, W. B. Saunders, Philadelphia, 1968.
'Stray dogs commit rape': *AABS*, vol. 13, (1–2), 1984, p. 113.
'Unsurprisingly, cats suffer': *Wildlife Research*, vol. 27, pp. 603–11; S. O'Brien, *Tears of the Cheetah: The Genetic Secrets of our Animal Ancestors*, St Martin's Press, New York, 2005.
'Some tomcats get so frustrated': *AB*, vol. 42, pp. 227–41.
'Male cats and dogs masturbate': *Behaviour*, vol. 18, 1961, pp. 1–24; *Vet. Clin. North Am.*, vol. 7 (4), 1977, p. 723; Beaver, *Veterinary Aspects of Feline Behaviour*, C. V. Mosby, St Louis, 1980, p. 133.
'In laboratory tests': *Behaviour*, vol. 18, 1961, pp. 1–24.

Whelp!: How Cats and Dogs Cope with Birth and Beyond (pages 98–101)

'Female cats can conceive from sex with several males':

Proceedings of the Royal Society B: Biological Sciences, no. 268, 2001, pp. 1049–53.

'Dogs have false pregnancies': Bruce Fogle, *Caring for Your Dog*, Dorling Kindersley, London, 2002, pp. 314–15.

'Cats act as midwives': *JFMS*, vol. 6, pp. 19–28.

'Fading Puppy Syndrome': Bruce Fogle, *Caring For Your Dog*, Dorling Kindersley, London, 2002, pp. 314–15; http://www.psych.qub.ac.uk/staff/teaching/hepper/profile/index.aspx.

'A female cat in labour can deliver': *Maternal Behaviour in Mammals*, H. L. Rheingold, John Wiley, New York, 1963.

'An average mother cat has between one and eight kittens per litter': G. Wood, *Animal Facts & Feats*, Doubleday, New York, 1972; Beaver, *Veterinary Aspects of Feline Behaviour*, C. V. Mosby, St Louis, 1980, p. 124; M. & F. Sunquist, *Wild Cats of the World*, University of Chicago Press, 2002, p. 110.

'Cat's milk contains': M. & F. Sunquist, *Wild Cats of the World*, University of Chicago Press, 2002, p. 109.

'Kittens double their birth weight': *Journal of Zoology*, vol. 213, 1987, pp. 153–79.

'For the first two to three weeks of their lives': *JAVMA*, vol. 140, p. 1076.

'In packs of feral dogs': Beaver, *Canine Behaviour: A Guide for Veterinarians*, W. B. Saunders, Philadelphia, 1999, p. 226.

'Male cats are sometimes child-killers': *Aggressive Behavior*, vol. 25, pp. 445–9; *AB*, vol. 45, pp. 13–23.

PART FIVE

EATS GOATS AND LEAVES: CANINE AND FELINE FOOD AND DRINK

'Given a choice, Beagles, Poodles and Basenjis': C. Thorne (ed.), *The Waltham Book of Cat and Dog Behaviour*, Pergamon Press, Oxford, 1992, pp. 124–5.

Cats Snack, Dogs Have Dinner: Why Both Are What Their Ancestors Ate (pages 107–18)

'Old eating habits die hard': *Journal of Nutrition*, vol. 136, pp. 1927S–31S.

'Dogs have forty-two teeth': C. Thorne (ed.), *The Waltham Book of Cat and Dog Behaviour*, Pergamon Press, Oxford, 1992. p. 33.

'Cats are experts at plucking feathers': Desmond Morris, *Catwatching*, Ebury Press, 2002, p. 54.

'Dogs have more taste-buds than cats': S. Coren, *How Dogs Think: Understanding the Canine Mind*, Pocket Books, London, 2005, p. 104.

'While, in general, canines are what scientists call neophilic': *Journal of Nutrition*, vol. 136, pp. 1927S–31S; *AABS*, vol. 68, pp. 257–68.

'Cats don't eat exactly the same thing': *AABS*, vol. 68, pp. 257–68.

'The cat's picky nature': *JFMS*, vol. 6, pp. 313–20.

'Cats are hypercarnivores': M. & F. Sunquist, *Wild Cats of the World*, University of Chicago Press, 2002, p. 5.

'As a result, cats' taste-buds': *Comparative Biochemistry and*

Physiology, vol. 114, pp. 205–9.
'Dogs . . . react to a sweet-tasting chemical called furaneol': S. Coren, *How Dogs Think: Understanding the Canine Mind*, Pocket Books, London, 2005, p. 106.
'Chocolate, for instance, can be poisonous': *Tierarztliche Praxis Ausgabe Kleintiere Heimtiere*, vol. 28, pp. 79–85; *Journal of the American Animal Hospital Association*, vol. 19, pp. 246–8.
'Raisins and grapes can also be fatal': *Journal of Veterinary Emergency and Critical Care*, vol. 14, no. 203, Sep. 2004.
'Cats don't like sweet things': *Comparative Biochemistry and Physiology*, vol. 114, pp. 205–9.
'Unlike humans, both dogs and cats can taste water': *Science*, vol. 171, pp. 699–701; S. Coren, *How Dogs Think: Understanding the Canine Mind*, Pocket Books, London, 2005, p. 108.
'The average dog takes in just over a litre of water a day': E. Hafez, *The Behaviour of Domestic Dogs*, Williams & Wilkins, Baltimore, 1969, p. 438.
'Cats have highly efficient kidneys': C. Thorne (ed.), *The Waltham Book of Cat and Dog Behaviour*, Pergamon Press, Oxford, 1992, p. 123.
'Some cats drink with their paws': Beaver, *Veterinary Aspects of Feline Behaviour*, C. V. Mosby, St Louis, 1980, p. 150.
'During hot weather': Beaver, *Canine Behaviour: A Guide for Veterinarians*, W. B. Saunders, Philadelphia, 1999, p. 244.
'Bitches are much more prone to obesity': *Journal of the American Animal Hospital Association*, vol. 14, p. 402.
'Puppies eat much less when they dine alone': *British Journal of*

Animal Behaviour, vol. 3, p. 131.
'Cats are much less likely to get overweight': Bruce Fogle, *The Cat's Mind*, Pelham Books, London, 1991, p. 127.
'Anorexia ... dogs can suffer from it': *Vet. Clin. North Am. (Small Animal. Pract.)*, vol. 12. no. 4, p. 683.
'Dogs on diets fight less': *AABS*, vol. 43, (1), p. 43
'Dogs eat faeces – and not just canine ones': *Vet. Clin. North Am. (Small Anim. Pract.)*, vol. 12, no. 4, p. 683, and vol. 21, no. 2, p. 281.
'Dogs can get cravings to eat the most bizarre things': *Vet. Clin. North Am. (Small Anim. Pract.)*, vol. 12, no. 4, p. 683.
'Dogs can become seriously ill': Bruce Fogle, *Caring for Your Dog*, Dorling Kindersley, London, 2002, p. 414.
'Many common garden plants and flowers are also poisonous': Bruce Fogle, *Caring For Your Dog*, Dorling Kindersley, London, 2002, p. 424.
'Dogs also poison themselves by drinking antifreeze': *Journal of the American Animal Hospital Association*, vol. 18, pp. 492–7.
'Onions, garlic and macadamia nuts are all poisonous to dogs': *Veterinary Clinical Pathology*, vol. 34, pp. 224–31; *Australian Veterinary Practitioner*, vol. 30, p. 6.
'Pet food is driving cat evolution': *AABS*, vol. 65, pp. 273–83.
'Dogs produce different types of saliva': S. Coren, *How Dogs Think: Understanding the Canine Mind*, Pocket Books, London, 2005, p. 103.
'The whiff of food on someone else's breath': *Behavioural Processes*, vol. 74, pp. 104–6.

'Contrary to the familiar saying, old dogs can learn new tricks': *Neurobiology of Aging*, January 2005, reported in *Science Daily*, 21 Jan. 2005.

'Black cats don't eat jelly': *Journal of Nutrition*, vol. 132, pp. 1646S–8S.

Kangaroo and Tortoise Eggs: What Cats and Dogs Eat in the Wild (pages 119–24)

'Dogs prey on a variety of animals': J. L. Long, *Introduced Mammals of the World*, CABI Publishing, 2003, p. 256.

'The kakapo': M. & F. Sunquist, *Wild Cats of the World*, University of Chicago Press, 2002, p. 105.

'Australian cats love possum': Bruce Fogle, *The Cat's Mind*, Pelham Books, London, 1991, p. 121.

'When domestic cats and dogs were introduced to the Turks and Caicos Islands': M. & F. Sunquist, *Wild Cats of the World*, University of Chicago Press, 2002, p. 105.

'Environmentalists in Australia blame cats': *NS*, vol. 142, no. 1926, 21 May 1994.

'An American study of more than 200 cats': *AABS*, vol. 93, (1–2), pp. 97–109.

'Cats are molecatchers': R. Tabor, *The Wild Life of the Domestic Cat*, Arrow Books, London, 1983.

'Cats can fish': Desmond Morris, *Catwatching*, Ebury Press, 2002, pp. 72–3.

'The most skilled angler': Smithsonian Institute: http://nationalzoo.si.edu/ConservationAndScience/SpotlightOn

Science/seidenstickerj20030526.cfm.
'Tom and Jerry aren't always natural enemies': *Journal of Mammalology*, vol. 75, 1994, pp. 24–38; *Elepaio*, vol. 54, (8), 1994, pp. 47–50.
'The Spanish introduced aggressive Bull Mastiffs': J. L. Long, *Introduced Mammals of the World*, CABI Publishing, 2003, p. 254.
'Cats are vampire hunters': *AABS*, vol. 39, pp. 141–50.
'Cannibalism is common in cats': *Journal Small Animal Practice*, vol. 14, July 1973, pp. 391–7; M. W. Fox, *Understanding Your Cat*, Coward, McCann & Geoghegan, New York, 1974.

Rex and Drugs: How Cats and Dogs Get High (pages 125–8)

'Cats can become addicted to hallucinogenic drugs': Desmond Morris, *Catwatching*, Ebury Press, 2002, pp. 92–3.
'In Japan, cats get high on the matatabi plant': *Wildlife Research*, vol. 21, pp. 389–99; Beaver, *Veterinary Aspects of Feline Behaviour*, C. V. Mosby, St Louis, 1980, p. 21.
'Addiction can run in the genes': *Journal of Heredity*, vol. 53, 1962, pp. 54–6.
'Catnip doesn't usually do any long-lasting damage': Desmond Morris, *Catwatching*, Ebury Press, 2002, pp. 92–3; Beaver, *Veterinary Aspects of Feline Behaviour*, C. V. Mosby, St Louis, 1980, p. 21.
'Catnip and matatabi are not the only plants': Beaver, *Veterinary*

Aspects of Feline Behaviour, C. V. Mosby, St Louis, 1980, p. 21; Desmond Morris, *Catwatching*, Ebury Press, 2002, pp. 92–3.

'If cats are given catnip or valerian internally they act as tranquillizers': Desmond Morris, *Catwatching*, Ebury Press, 2002, pp. 92–3.

'Dogs get high on cannabis': *Veterinary Record*, 11 Apr. 1992, reported in *NS*, vol. 134, no. 1821, 16 May 1992.

'Dogs are addictive to humans': Beaver, *Canine Behaviour: A Guide for Veterinarians*, W. B. Saunders, Philadelphia, 1999.

PART SIX

How Lassie Comes Home and Tom Always Lands on His Feet: Cats and Dogs in Motion

Making Tracks: How Cats and Dogs Put One Paw in Front of Another (pages 133–7)

'Puppies take their first tentative steps': *Journal of Comparative Physiology Psychology*, vol. 45, 1952, p. 329.

'All cats are digitigrade': M. & F. Sunquist, *Wild Cats of the World*, University of Chicago Press, 2002, p. 5.

'The cat has a symmetrical walk': J. Gray, *Animal Locomotion*, W. W. Norton, New York, 1968.

'Cats normally walk at around 0.9 metres a second': J. Gray, *Animal Locomotion*, W. W. Norton, New York, 1968; P. P. Gambaryan, *How Mammals Run*, John Wiley, New York, 1974.

References

'As they move through the gears': P. P. Gambaryan, *How Mammals Run*, John Wiley, New York, 1974.

'Most breeds of domestic cat can reach speeds of up to 30 mph': *Natural History*, March 1974; *The Cornell Book of Cats: A Comprehensive Medical Reference for Every Cat and Kitten*, Villard Books, 1989.

'Walking backwards is an awkward-looking process': *Journal of Biomechanics*, vol. 33, (8), Aug. 2000, pp. 911–16.

'Some 84 per cent of dogs go for a run when they are let off the leash': *JAVMA*, vol. 207, no. 2, p. 186.

'Galloping dogs breathe at the same rate they run': *SCI*, vol. 219, 1983, p. 251.

'Because of their lack of large numbers of sweat glands': *AABS*, vol. 81, no. 2, 2003, pp. 149–61.

'Dogs pant 200 times a minute': C. Thorne (ed.), *The Waltham Book of Cat and Dog Behaviour*, Pergamon Press, Oxford, 1992, p. 35.

'Scientists have discovered that a dog refrigerates its brain': *Science*, vol. 195, issue 4280, 25 Feb. 1977, pp. 781–3.

'Young puppies can't shiver': *American Journal of Physiology*, vol. 183, p. 340.

'Cats instinctively react to cold': *Arch. Int. Physiol. Biochem.*, vol. 84, Oct. 1976, pp. 787–99.

'Greyhounds can reach speeds of just under 40 mph': Beaver, *Canine Behaviour: A Guide for Veterinarians*, W. B. Saunders, Philadelphia, 1999, p. 294, *Natural History*, March 1974.

'Sled dogs are marathon champions': R. Coppinger, & R. Schneider, 'Evolution of working dogs', in J. A. Serpell (ed.),

The Domestic Dog: Its Evolution, Behaviour and Interactions with People, Cambridge University Press, 1995.

'Racing sled dogs are most active around sunrise and sunset': *AABS*, vol. 15, no. 2, p. 161.

'Offered a ride on a fire engine': *Nature*, vol. 144, no. 3650, 1939, p. 671.

'Dogs are capable of mastering': Beaver, *Canine Behaviour: A Guide for Veterinarians*, W. B. Saunders, Philadelphia, 1999, p. 296.

They Fly Through the Air with the Greatest of Ease: How Cats and Dogs Defy Gravity (pages 138–43)

'In 1987 two vets': *JAVMA*, vol. 191, 1987, pp. 1399–403; *Ann. Emerg. Med.*, vol. 15, 1986, pp. 1088–93.

'The most remarkable survivor': *JAVMA*, vol. 191, 1987, pp. 1399–1403.

'Cats that fall from higher altitudes': *Natural History*, Aug. 1989, pp. 20–6.

'The cat owes its amazing ability to survive falls': *Nature*, vol. 332, 14 Apr. 1988, pp. 586–7; C. Thorne (ed.), *The Waltham Book of Cat and Dog Behaviour*, Pergamon Press, Oxford, 1992, p. 37.

'For many years the cat's self-righting ability': *La Nature*, no. 1119, 10 Nov. 1894, pp. 369–70; http://www.verrueckte-experimente.de/leseproben_e.html.

'Cats are so good at landing on their feet that damaged jaws': M. Pollard, *The Encyclopedia of Cats*, Paragon, 1999.

'Cats are born with the ability to right themselves': D. C. Turner & P. Bateson (eds), *The Domestic Cat: The Biology of its Behaviour*, Cambridge University Press, 1988; C. Thorne (ed.), *The Waltham Book of Cat and Dog Behaviour*, Pergamon Press, Oxford, 1992, p. 56.

'Small dogs that fall from buildings are prone to more serious injuries than cats': *Nature*, vol. 332, 14 Apr. 1988, pp. 586–7.

'Dogs can parachute too': Imperial War Museum; http://www.iwm.org.uk/upload/package/74/AnimalsWar/press.htm.

The Lassie Principle: How Cats and Dogs Usually Find Their Way Home (pages 144–50)

'Long before Disney': *Science*, vol. 56, no. 1447, Sep. 1922, p. 339.

'A blind Cocker Spaniel': *CP*, vol. 19, (2), p. 20.

'Cats frequently track down owners': *Daily Express*, 23 Apr. 2007; *Journal of Parapsychology*, vol. 26, pp. 1–22.

'Cats seem to sense families are moving home': *Journal of Parapsychology*, vol. 26, pp. 1–22.

'An American scientist, Francis Herrick': *The Scientific Monthly*, vol. 14, no. 6, June 1922, pp. 525–39.

'Cats definitely have an excellent sense of direction': Bruce Fogle, *The Cat's Mind*, Pelham Books, London, 1991, p. 48; Desmond Morris, *Catwatching*, Ebury Press, 2002, pp. 94–5.

'Some scientists believe cats are so sensitive': Bruce Fogle, *The Cat's Mind*, Pelham Books, London, 1991, p. 48; Morris, ibid.

'In the American maze experiments': Bruce Fogle, ibid; Morris, ibid.

'Some scientists think dogs use': *CP*, vol. 19, (2) p. 20; J. Perlson, *The Dog: An Historical, Psychological and Personality Study*, Vantage Press, New York, 1968.

'There is no shortage of controversial theories': Sheldrake, *Dogs That Know When Their Owners Are Coming Home*, Hutchinson, London, 1999; *Discover*, vol. 21, no. 8, Aug. 2000, pp 60–5.

'Dogs that roam or run away': *JAVMA*, 1976, vol. 31, (3–4), p. 294.

'Dogs don't always arrive home safely, unfortunately': *JAVMA*, vol. 167, (10), 1975, p. 938; vol. 164, (5), 1974, p. 499.

'Cats by contrast, benefit not from their ability': *Animal Welfare*, vol. 13, no. 1, Feb. 2004, pp. 51–5.

Fat Cats Can't Jump: Why Some Cats and Dogs Don't Get Around So Well (pages 151–3)

'Cats get stuck up trees': M. Pollard, *The Encyclopedia of Cats*, Paragon, 1999.

'Fat, stubby cats can't jump': *Journal of Experimental Biology*, vol. 205, no. 24, Dec. 2002, pp. 3877–89.

'Dogs aren't always in control of their movements': P. J. B. Slater, *Essentials of Animal Behaviour*, Cambridge University Press, 1999.

'Dogs are born with an equivalent of a thumb': Bruce Fogle, *Caring for Your Dog*, Dorling Kindersley, London, 2002, p. 58.

'Elderly dogs aren't so good at finding home': Beaver, *Canine Behaviour: A Guide for Veterinarians*, W. B. Saunders, Philadelphia, 1999, p. 278.

'Cats don't have collar bones': *Acta Anatomica*, vol. 154, (2), pp. 128–34.

PART SEVEN

THE CAT PACK: THE SOCIAL LIVES OF CATS AND DOGS

12.4 Children: The Family Life of Cats and Dogs (pages 159–63)

'Tomcats have a bad reputation as parents': *Advances in Ethology* (supplement to *Ethology*), vol. 28, pp. 1–66; *Veterinary Clinics of North America: Small Animal Practice*, vol. 27, pp. 549–68.

'Siamese dads take more interest': M. Beadle, *The Cat: History, Biology and Behaviour*, Simon & Schuster, New York, 1977.

'Cat mothers teach their young how to kill their prey': *The Quarterly Review of Biology*, vol. 67, pp. 151–74.

'Kittens know their mothers really do know best': *Science*, vol. 166, pp. 901–3.

'Young dogs and cats learn not to kill their friends': Leyhausen, *Motivations of Human and Animal Behaviour: An Ethological View*, Van Nostrand Reinhold & Coppinger, New York, 1973, p. 116.

'Dogs don't forget their mother': *AB*, vol. 34, pp. 288–9.

'Wild dogs make better fathers': *AZ*, vol. 25, 1985, p. 853.

'Dogs make natural foster parents': *Canine*, vol. 7 (1), p. 10.

Leaders of the Pack: How Cats, Dogs and Other Animals Live Together (pages 164–70)

'Feral dogs form gangs': C. Gentry, *When Dogs Run Wild: The Sociology of Feral Dogs and Wildlife*, McFarland, Jefferson, NC, 1983.

'Leadership within a feral gang is tested regularly': C. Gentry, ibid.

'Domestic dogs that are allowed to roam free': C. Gentry, ibid.

'Cats are far from the solitary creatures': D. C. Turner & P. Bateson (eds), *The Domestic Cat: The Biology of its Behaviour* (2nd ed.), Cambridge University Press, 1988, p. 121.

'In colonies, cats greet each other by touching noses': *JFMS*, vol. 6, pp. 19–28.

'Higher-ranking cats tend to groom lower-ranking cats': *Journal of Ethology*, vol. 16, no. 1, 1998, pp. 1–13.

'Grooming calms cats down': M. W. Fox, *Understanding Your Cat*, Coward, McCann & Geoghegan, New York, 1974.

'Cats signal aggression': *Acta Zoologica Fennica*, vol. 171, pp. 83–8.

'It's a woman's world – at least, if you are a cat': *JFMS*, vol. 6, pp. 19–28.

'Cats make friends and enemies': *JFMS*, vol. 6, pp. 19–28.

'Female cats are freer spirits': *Journal of Animal Ecology*, vol. 72, pp. 203–11.

'Cats can be bullies and thieves': *JFMS*, vol. 6, pp. 19–28.

'Cats and dogs can also form strange partnerships': Press Association, 2 Feb. 2006.

'A Chihuahua in China': Press Association, 10 Mar. 2005.

'Dogs will allow the offspring': Press Association, 21 Apr. 2005; 5 May 2005.

'A dog and a giant black bear': Burghardt, *The Genesis of Animal Play*, p. 88.

'Cats are not intimidated by bigger animals': *BBC News*, http://news.bbc.co.uk/1/hi/world/americas/5067912.stm.

'Cats and dogs don't necessarily fight all the time': *AABS*, vol. 30, p. 351.

'Dog breeds that have been trained to work with livestock': Beaver, *Canine Behaviour: A Guide for Veterinarians*, W. B. Saunders, Philadelphia, 1999, p. 178.

Bosom Buddies: How Cats and Dogs Evolved into Man's Best Friends (pages 171–8)

'Dogs are more closely related to sea-lions': A. Ruvinsky & J. Sampson (eds), *The Genetics of the Dog*, CABI, Oxfordshire, 2001, pp. 2–3.

'The most recent DNA studies': *Science*, vol. 276, pp. 1687–9; *Science*, vol. 298, pp. 1613–16; A. Ruvinsky & J. Sampson (eds), *The Genetics of the Dog*, CABI, Oxfordshire, 2001; *New York Times*, 4 Feb. 2007.

'A grave in Ein Mallaha': *Nature*, vol. 276, pp. 608–10, 1978.

'The earliest archaeological evidence of dogs in Europe': S. Davis, *The Archaeology of Animals*, Yale University Press, 1987.

'The widespread belief is that wolves evolved into dogs': R. & L. Coppinger, *Dogs, A New Understanding of Canine Origin, Behavior and Evolution*, University of Chicago, 2002; *Science*, vol. 298, pp. 1540–2.

'By contrast, cats': *Biological Journal of the Linnean Society*, vol. 75, pp. 361–6.

'Cats also originated in Asia': *Science*, vol. 298, pp. 1613–16.

'All thirty-eight members of the modern cat family': D. C. Turner & P. Bateson (eds), *The Domestic Cat: The Biology of its Behaviour*, Cambridge University Press, 1988, p. 180.

'The earliest evidence of cats': D. C. Turner & P. Bateson (eds), *The Domestic Cat: The Biology of its Behaviour*, Cambridge University Press, 1988, p. 183.

'Dogs . . . all but one of the earth's continents, Antarctica': C. Thorne (ed.), *The Waltham Book of Cat and Dog Behaviour*, Pergamon Press, Oxford, 1992, p. 2.

'According to one study, all 701 modern breeds of dog': Annual Meeting of the American Association for the Advancement of Science in Seattle, Washington, 2004, reported in *New Scientist*, online, 16 Feb. 2004.

'American breeds of dog': *Science*, vol. 298, pp. 1613–16.

'The first domesticated cats': Beadle, *The Cat: History, Biology and Behaviour*, Collins & Harvill Press, London, 1977.

'The Egyptians revered both cats and dogs': D. C. Turner & P. Bateson (eds), *The Domestic Cat: The Biology of its Behaviour*, Cambridge University Press, 1988, p. 185.

'The export of cats was illegal': Beadle, *The Cat: History,*

Biology and Behaviour, Collins & Harvill Press, London, 1977.

'In 50 BC, the historian Diodorus Siculus': D. C. Turner & P. Bateson (eds), *The Domestic Cat: The Biology of its Behaviour*, Cambridge University Press, 1988, p. 185.

'The Egyptians bred cats specifically': *NS*, vol. 185, no. 2485, 8 Feb. 2005.

'The ancient Libyans': D. C. Turner & P. Bateson (eds), *The Domestic Cat: The Biology of its Behaviour*, Cambridge University Press, 1988, p. 184.

'The Greeks loved their dogs': Zeuner, *A History of Domesticated Animals*, Hutchinson, London, 1963.

'The Romans weren't much taken by cats': Beadle, *The Cat: History, Biology and Behaviour*, 1977; Zeuner, *A History of Domesticated Animals*, Hutchinson, London, 1963.

'The Romans produced the first "Beware of the Dog" signs': J. Perlson, *The Dog: An Historical, Psychological and Personality Study*, Vantage Press, New York, 1968.

'The Romans were the first to use dogs as guide dogs': *Survey of Ophthalmology*, vol. 48, pp. 452–8.

'You could call them bosom buddies': Marion Schwartz, *A History of Dogs in the Early Americas*, Yale University Press, 1997.

'Cats only moved to the Americas': C. Thorne (ed.), *The Waltham Book of Cat and Dog Behaviour*, Pergamon Press, Oxford, 1992, p. 6.

'Wild dingoes are actually descendants': *Science*, vol. 298, no. 5598, 22 Nov. 2002.

'By contrast, the Polynesian dog, or kuri': J. L. Long, *Introduced Mammals of the World*, CABI Publishing, 2003, p. 254.

Soul Mates: Why Cats, Dogs and Humans Are Made for Each Other (pages 179–87)

'Dogs are much better at understanding humans': *Science*, vol. 298, no. 5598, pp. 1634–6.

'Dogs also know when . . . to beg': *Behavioural Processes*, vol. 66, pp. 161–72.

'Dogs, it seems, are highly tuned to their master's voice': *AABS*, vol. 91, (1–2), pp. 129–41.

'Poodles and humans, for instance, share 75 per cent': *Science*, vol. 301, pp. 1898–1903.

'Both dogs and cats can follow human pointing gestures': *JCP*, vol. 119, pp. 179–86; *JCP*, vol. 116, pp. 27–34.

'Dogs rely more on humans for help than cats do': *JCP*, vol. 119, pp. 179–86.

'Cats and humans have very similar neurological systems': *JFMS*, vol. 8, pp. 234–42.

'Cats also led scientists to isolating a natural brain chemical': *Science*, vol. 276, pp. 1265–8.

'A dog's brain is also very similar': S. Coren, *How Dogs Think: Understanding the Canine Mind*, Pocket Books, London, 2005, pp. 6–7.

'Dogs and humans are the only animals with prostates': American Cancer Society, 2 Aug. 1999, www.cancer.org.

'Cats and dogs are good for human health': *NS*, vol. 140, no. 1894, 9 Oct. 1993.

'Numerous scientific studies': *Anthrozoos*, vol. 18, p. 496.

'Dogs improve people's social lives': *British Journal of Psychology*, vol. 91, pp. 61–70.

'Dogs bring out the maternal instincts in women': *Ethology*, vol. 112, no. 1, Jan. 2006, pp. 64–73.

'A study in 1995': *British Psychological Society, Research Digest*, 29 Mar. 2006 (http://bps-research-digest.blogspot.com/2006/03/reasons-to-own-dog.html).

'One study claimed that dogs have a more positive influence': *British Journal of Health Psychology*, 22 Jan. 2007.

'One study at the Keck School of Medicine': *Science Daily*, 29 Aug. 2006.

'Living with cats increases young children's risks of getting eczema': American Thoracic Society, International Conference, 21 May 2006, reported in *Science Daily*, 22 May 2006.

'In an Australian study': *Epidemiology and Infection*, vol. 134, pp. 926–34.

'Cats and dogs in the main live happily': Beaver, *Canine Behaviour: A Guide for Veterinarians*, W. B. Saunders, Philadelphia, 1999, p. 181.

'In 1991, the US Centers for Disease Control and Prevention': *NS*, vol. 142, no. 1930, 18 June 1994.

'Do dogs suffer from the Curse of the Werewolfhound?': *British Medical Journal*, vol. 331, p. 1278, 26 Nov. 2005, doi:10.1136/bmj.331.7527.1278.

'Domestic cats are as likely to attack their owner': D. C. Turner & P. Bateson (eds), *The Domestic Cat: The Biology of its Behaviour*, Cambridge University Press, 1988, p. 221.

PART EIGHT

Dr Labradoodle: How Cats and Dogs Have Become Breeds Apart

Cats Aren't From Mars: Some Odd Truths About Cat and Dog Breeds (pages 193–200)

'The Romans were dog lovers': J. Clutton-Brock, *Domesticated Animals from Early Times*, University of Texas Press, Austin, 1981.

'The basic construction of a dog's skeleton is the same': C. Thorne (ed.), *The Waltham Book of Cat and Dog Behaviour*, Pergamon Press, Oxford, 1992, p. 31.

'Cats and dogs have similar numbers of vertebrae': C. Thorne (ed.), *The Waltham Book of Cat and Dog Behaviour*, Pergamon Press, Oxford, 1992, p. 32; R. Robinson, *Genetics for Cat Breeders*, Penguin Press, 1991.

'Dogs that look like wolves behave like them': *New Scientist*, vol. 153, no. 2075, 29 Mar. 1997.

'Some breeds don't grow up': *New Scientist*, vol. 153, no. 2075, 29 Mar. 1997; *AB*, vol. 53, pp. 297–304.

'One of the most popular breeds of cat': www.ragdollcats.com/history.htm.

'Pet dogs are worse at dealing with problems': *Anthrozoos*,

vol. 10, pp. 214–24.
'Feline personalities fall into three categories': *AB*, vol. 61, pp. 231–7.
'Different dog breeds have different personalities': B. L. & L. A. Hart, 'Selecting pet dogs on the basis of cluster analysis of breed behaviour profiles and gender', *JAVMA*, 1985, vol. 186, pp. 1181–5.
'Cats according to different personality traits': Bruce Fogle, *The Cat's Mind*, Pelham Books, London, 1991.

Some Pets Get All the Bad Luck: Breeds That Draw the Genetic Short Straw (pages 201–13)

'A major study by the American Kennel Club': *New York Times*, 4 Feb. 2007.
'Of the 170 breeds of dog registered': *NS*, vol. 144, no. 1950, 5 Nov. 1994.
'No wonder so many dogs are called Spot': Bruce Fogle, *Caring for Your Dog*, Dorling Kindersley, London, 2002, pp. 198–9.
'Some 30 per cent of Dalmatians': *Science Daily*, 10 Feb. 2005.
'Half of Rottweilers and Miniature Schnauzers are short-sighted': *Invest. Ophthalmol. Vis. Sci.*, vol. 33, pp. 2459–63.
'The Bengal has an unusual affinity for water': D. Rice, *Bengal Cats: Everything About Purchase, Care, Nutrition, Health Care and Behaviour*, Barron's Educational Series, 2005.
'Dalmatians get a kind of gout': www.VeterinaryPartner.com.
'Dogs suffer from the only known contagious cancer': *Cell*, vol. 126, p. 477.

'Cats get asthma': *National Geographic News*, 25 Oct. 2005.

'Dogs can develop strange, obsessional habits': A. Ruvinsky & J. Sampson (eds), *The Genetics of the Dog*, CABI, Oxfordshire, 2001; *New York Times*, 4 Feb. 2007.

'Feral dogs are less prone to infectious diseases': Bruce Fogle, *Caring for Your Dog*, Dorling Kindersley, London, 2002, p. 101.

'Other medical conditions common in particular breeds include': This section was compiled from information in the following books: A. Ruvinsky & J. Sampson (eds), *The Genetics of the Dog*, CABI, Oxfordshire, 2001; Beaver, *Canine Behaviour: A Guide for Veterinarians*, W. B. Saunders, Philadelphia, 1999; Bruce Fogle, *Caring for Your Dog*, Dorling Kindersley, London, 2002; J. Fennell, *The Seven Ages of Man's Best Friend*, HarperCollins, London, 2005; D. Taylor, *The British Veterinary Association Guide to Dog Care*, Dorling Kindersley, 1989.

'Dogs that resemble wolves live longer': S. Coren, *How Dogs Think: Understanding the Canine Mind*, Pocket Books, London, 2005, p. 335.

'The most authoritative study of canine lifespans in the UK': *Veterinary Record, The Journal of the British Veterinary Association*, Nov. 1999.

'The oldest dog on record': *Advantage*, vol. 1, (1), p. 2.

'The oldest recorded cat': M. & F. Sunquist, *Wild Cats of the World*, University of Chicago Press, 2002, p. 110.

'Toyger': *TICA, The International Cat Association, List of Recognized Breeds*, Apr. 2007.

'The modern passion for breeding dogs': *New York Times*, 4 Feb. 2007.

You Are What You Wear: How Cats and Dogs Are Colour-Coded (pages 214–17)

'White, roan and piebald dogs are more likely to be deaf': S. Coren, *How Dogs Think: Understanding the Canine Mind*, Pocket Books, London, 2005, p. 57.
'Tortoiseshell cats inherit the ginger patches': *NS*, online, 10 May 2003.
'Male cats with coloured coats are rare': *AB*, vol. 42, pp. 227–41; *AB*, vol. 40, pp. 183–6.
'Not all white cats with blue eyes are deaf': *Journal of Heredity*, vol. 62, p. 171.
'Black cats shouldn't be seen as symbols of bad luck': *Current Biology*, vol. 13, pp. 448–53.
'Black cats are more tolerant': *Scientific American*, vol. 237 (5), pp. 100–7.
'Red spells danger': *AABS*, vol. 47, pp. 75–89.
'A study of eighty-four British Shorthair kittens': *Proceedings of the 30th International Congress of the ISAE*, p. 112.
'Cats with orange in their coat': D. C. Turner & P. Bateson (eds), *The Domestic Cat: The Biology of its Behaviour*, Cambridge University Press, 1988, p. 53.

PART NINE

It's a Cat and Dog's Life: Some Curious Truths About Canine and Feline Lifestyles

All That Litters: Personal Hygiene in Cats and Dogs (pages 223–8)

'Male and female dogs have very different toiletary habits': Beaver, *Canine Behaviour: A Guide for Veterinarians*, W. B. Saunders, Philadelphia, 1999, p. 269.
'The cat's fastidious nature': Beaver, *Veterinary Aspects of Feline Behaviour*, C. V. Mosby, St Louis, 1980, pp. 167–8.
'Cats that bury their faeces are insecure': Desmond Morris, *Catwatching*, Ebury Press, 2002, p. 24.
'Cats soil their owner's home': Beaver, *Veterinary Aspects of Feline Behaviour*, C. V. Mosby, St Louis, 1980, pp. 170–1.
'A male cat's wee is smellier than that of a female': *Comparative Biochemistry and Physiology*, vol. 112B, pp. 581–8.
'The average dog deposits': Beck, *The Ecology of Stray Dogs, A Study of Free-Ranging Urban Animals*, York Press, Baltimore, 1973.
'In Britain alone, dogs deposit 4.5 million litres of urine': *NS*, vol. 140, no. 1894, 9 Oct. 1993.
'Dogs are highly regular': Beaver, *Canine Behaviour: A Guide for Veterinarians*, W. B. Saunders, Philadelphia, 1999, p. 276.
'A study of Beagles': *Behavior*, vol. 47, 1973, p. 257.
'Cats expend almost as much bodily fluid': www.messybeast.com/towards-end.htm.
'It's not surprising that cat owners get covered in cat hair':

M. Pollard, *The Encyclopedia of Cats*, Parragon, 1999.
'Castrated male cats grow their hair long': *Journal of Genetics*, vol. 49, pp. 214–20.
'Dogs have two types of hair': Bruce Fogle, *Caring for Your Dog*, Dorling Kindersley, London, 2002, p. 176.
'Dogs go bald': P. McKeever & R. Harvey, *Skin Diseases of the Dog and Cat*, Iowa State University Press, 1998; *Washington Post*, 8 June 2004, p. C10.
'Dogs suffer from dandruff': P. McKeever & R. Harvey, *Skin Diseases of the Dog and Cat*, Iowa State University Press, 1998.
'Cats attract more fleas than dogs do': *Veterinary Record*, vol. 160, no. 15, 14 Apr. 2007, pp. 503–6.
'Dogs also suffer from DO': Bruce Fogle, *Caring for Your Dog*, Dorling Kindersley, London, 2002, p. 195.
'Cats lose their hair when they are stressed': *Journal of Psychosomatic Research*, vol. 7, pp. 229–35.
'Cats can also get eczema': M. Fox, *Abnormal Behavior in Animals*, W. B. Saunders, Philadelphia, 1968.
'Hairballs make cats depressed': *Feline Practice*, vol. 6, p. 14, July 1976.

Bite Me: How Cats and Dogs Play (pages 229–34)

'Young domestic dogs are much more playful': *AZ*, vol. 14, 1974, p. 323.
'The response is positive 77 per cent of the time': *AZ*, vol. 14, 1974, p. 323.

'Lots of puppies play at mounting one another': *AZ*, vol. 14, 1974, p. 323.

'A signal in dogs that means "let's play at fighting"': Burghardt, *The Genesis of Animal Play*, p. 91.

'Puppies rarely play on their own': *AZ*, vol. 14, 1974, p. 323.

'Puppies bit each other in 87 per cent of their games': *AZ*, vol. 14, 1974, p. 323.

'Cats start playing at two weeks of age': E. Hafez, *The Behaviour of Domestic Animals*, Williams & Wilkins, Baltimore, 1975.

'At between four and sixteen weeks of age cats take part in complex social play': *AZ*, vol. 14, 1974, pp. 427–36.

'Cats also play individual games': *AZ*, vol. 14, pp. 427–36.

'Adult cats hunt for fun': Bruce Fogle, *The Cat's Mind*, Pelham Books, London, 1991, p. 123.

'Dogs need mental stimulation': *Animal Welfare*, vol. 13, no. 3, Aug. 2004, pp. 367–73.

'Cats play more with toys when they are hungry': *AABS*, vol. 58, (1–2), pp. 143–50.

'When dogs play with humans': *AABS*, vol. 6, (3), pp. 235–48.

'Dogs are good winners but bad losers': *AABS*, vol. 75, pp. 161–76.

The Joy of Rex: Some Things That Make Cats and Dogs Happy (and Sad) (pages 235–41)

'Cats develop stress-related illnesses': *Science Daily*, 27 Oct. 2004.

'Cats hate unpredictability': *AABS*, vol. 38, pp. 143–58.

'Cats also get stressed by rejection': Animal Behavior Society, Utah, reported in *NS* online, 17 Aug. 2006.

'Dogs laugh': Animal Behavior Society conference, Corvallis, Oregon, 14–18 July 2001.

'Dogs like the sound of laughter': Proceedings of the 7th International Conference on Environmental Enrichment, 31 July–5 Aug. 2005.

'Dogs respond to the sound of human whispers': *AABS*, vol. 66, pp. 235–48.

'Cats don't laugh': D. C. Turner & P. Bateson (eds), *The Domestic Cat: The Biology of its Behaviour*, p. 233; wikipedia.

'Having the television on in the background': *Animal Welfare*, vol. 14, no. 2, May 2005, pp. 143–8.

'One scientist cites the case of a dog-care centre': S. Coren, *How Dogs Think: Understanding the Canine Mind*, Pocket Books, London, 2005, p. 36.

'Whereas dogs like Westerns': *Animal Welfare*, vol. 14, no. 2, May 2005, pp. 143–8; *Psychological Science*, vol. 4, 1993, pp. 54–7.

'The sound of Bach': *Animal Welfare*, vol. 11, p. 385; *NS* online, 23 Oct. 2002.

'Bach, yes; barking, no': *Journal of Applied Animal Welfare Science*, vol. 4 (4), pp. 257–70.

Play It Again, Tom: When Cats Play Piano, Dogs Howl Along (pages 242–5)

'Cats make musical instruments': *Musical Quarterly*, vol. 75, no. 4, pp. 37–47.

'Cats and dogs featured in musical compositions': *Musical Quarterly*, ibid.

'Cats can compose music': *Musical Quarterly*, ibid.

'Cats can "play" piano': *Daily Mail*, 23 Apr. 2007.

'You could call it perfect bitch': S. Coren, *How Dogs Think: Understanding the Canine Mind*, Pocket Books, London, 2005, p. 312.

'Some famous musicians': S. Coren, *How Dogs Think: Understanding the Canine Mind*, Pocket Books, London, 2005, p. 314.

'Cats paint': Heather Busch and Burton Silver, *Why Cats Paint*, Weidenfeld & Nicolson, London, 1994.

'Dogs create their own masterpieces too': *Showbuzz*, CBS News online, 15 Apr. 2007.

Let Sleeping Dogs Snore: How Cats and Dogs Catch Forty Winks (pages 246–8)

'Cats sleep for two thirds of their lives': Bruce Fogle, *The Cat's Mind*, Pelham Books, London, 1991, p. 19.

'Cats dream': Bruce Fogle, *The Cat's Mind*, Pelham Books, London, 1991, p. 20.

'Some dogs are narcoleptic': *Nature Genetics*, vol. 23, pp. 3–4.

'Dogs also dream': *Australian Veterinary Practitioner*, vol. 21, pp. 144–7.

References

'Some 21 per cent of dogs snore': Unpublished study, Mayo Clinic Sleep Disorders Centre, http://www.mayoclinic.org/news/.